Simple Secrets to
Successful Northern Gardening

by Neil Moran

Copyright 1995
by Neil Moran and
Avery Color Studios
Reprinted 1997

Published by
Avery Color Studios
Marquette, Michigan 49855

Printed by
Lake Superior Press
Marquette, Michigan

ISBN 0-932212-87-5
Library of Congress Card No. 95-079339

What Others Say About *North Country Gardening:*

"In 'North Country Gardening,' Moran shares what he's learned about gardening in harsh climates and offers encouragement for those who think it can't possibly be done. He peppers his advice with humor and includes sections on soil preparation, animal control, specific plant choices and sources for supplies."

Karen Wittwer
Garden Writer, *Duluth News-Tribune*

"You can't help but get a kick out of his descriptions of certain season-stretching techniques, such as starting tender annuals early in a portable bed—in one case, a bird bath—that can be carted to the garage if the TV meteorologist utters that dreaded phrase, 'chance of frost tonight.'"

Marty Hair
Detroit Free Press Garden Writer

"The author's passion for gardening shows in his writing, which is wry, humorous and down-to-earth. Accompanying the easy-to-read text are many charts, diagrams and photos, making this a book that will be returned to time and again."

Deidre S. Tomaszewski
Sault Ste. Marie Evening News

"There is a dearth of good gardening books on dealing specifically with our long, cold winters and wet, cool summers. Among the better known gardening books for northern gardeners were those written by the late Leon Snyder, longtime University of Minnesota horticulturist... now there is another, titled 'North Country Gardening: Simple Secrets to Successful Northern Gardening.'"

Darrel Koehler
Grand Forks Herald

"Gardener-magazine writer Neil Moran has come out with his first book of gardening, 'North Country Gardening'... he knows of what he writes. Moran lives near Sault Ste. Marie, and despite the weather, has learned how to grow everything from tomatoes to cantaloupes. He shares with his readers those lessons, adding to them the advice of other gardening experts."

Marg Duford, Staff Writer
Traverse City Record Eagle

North Country Gardening

by Neil Moran

ABLE OF CONTENTS

DEDICATION

To the memory of Jane Louise Moran

Your love and encouragement
are with me always.

and to

My wife Sherri and children Kimmy & Trisha
whose patience and encouragement made
this endeavor possible.

INTRODUCTION

I spent my growing-up years gardening in the rich, fertile soil of Michigan's Thumb Area. The summer days were long and hot (and often dry); the nights were usually warm, and the corn as tall as trees. There isn't much you can't grow in this region unless you have a hankering for fresh coconuts or bananas.

When I was still in my teens my brother and I planted a huge garden. In this warm "southern" climate everything flourished: beefsteak tomatoes, Illini Extra Sweet Corn and even eggplant. It was with this naiveté, disguised as confidence, that I moved to the Upper Peninsula of Michigan and started gardening. I planted everything from lima beans to hubbard squash that first year, while neighbors looked on as if I was from another planet.

Miraculously, most of what I grew that summer ripened; it had been an un-usually long, hot summer. This gave me the confidence I needed to march blindly forward. Unfortunately, I was headed for disappointment. Over the last several years I've had to face the realities of gardening in this harsh climate: frosts in late June causing delays in planting—or worse, killing off young plants; and frost as early as the third week of August, bringing my flourishing corn and squash to a screeching halt.

Many times in the spring the ground would be so cold and wet that a green scum would form over the top of it just when I should have been planting. And don't forget the wind; "Alberta Clippers" from Canada punished my transplants. And alas, raccoons robbed my corn patch and deer snatched my squash.

Despite these difficulties, I've been able to grow just about everything in our cold weather climate. Admittedly, I haven't grown the extra sweet, sweet corn that requires a whopping 85 days of good growing weather; nor thick, juicy mouth watering beefsteak tomatoes commonly grown in the southern states; rather, I've experimented with varieties I've carefully chosen from select seed catalogs and nursery folks who start their plants in the northern region. And I've practiced various season extending methods to lengthen the growing season.

The corn I grow is just as fresh and nearly as tasty as any of the southern varieties, although not quite as large. And my tomatoes . . . well, I've failed to grow ripe ones on more than a few occasions. But what the heck, it gives us northerners a challenge; it builds character to take on the tomato year after year!

Compared to vegetables, flowers are easy to grow in the North. The moist rich earth in most areas is ideal for many varieties of perennials and annuals. Still, there are varieties that do much better than others because they are known to be hardy in the cold climates. I've compiled a list of flowers, such as columbine and lupine, which are particularly suitable to the area.

Likewise, there are many trees and shrubs suitable for this region. The big challenge is getting them through the winter. I've offered some tips on meeting this challenge which I've learned from experience and in talking to professional landscapers and county extension agents in different states throughout the region.

During the course of this book, I'll not only take you down my corn and potato rows, sharing my experiences along the way, but we'll journey to other parts of the North Country. I don't pretend to know everything about gardening in the cold climates. That's why I've asked many of you to tell me your secrets and share your season extending ideas that you use to ripen your produce and maintain beautiful trees, shrubs and flowers year after year.

I've asked you to share your knowledge because I know there's no typical northern climate. Each area in the North is unique in regard to soil, weather, proximity to water and number of frost free days. For example, the cool air that blows off the Great Lakes may be detrimental to your quest to grow a red ripe tomato. However, it's the warm air that moderates temperatures and prevents the late spring frosts common inland. Likewise, it gets downright chilly in the Green Mountains of Vermont, but this cold air is not as detrimental as the frost which tends to drop into the valleys below.

Similarly, soil types vary dramatically in the North. While sand and clay are predominant soil types in the northern region, folks living near river beds and valleys are gardening in a rich, albeit acid (from the predominance of coniferous trees in this region) sandy loam soil. You'll learn how to rise above these difficulties to grow the attractive and productive garden you've longed for.

Our lives are getting more hectic even here in the North. Folks can't waste time planting flowers, trees and shrubs only to see them succumb to the harsh elements. Unfortunately, most garden books and magazines don't offer advice to folks who still have snow on the ground in May! Hopefully, by following some of the tips in this book you can save time and money by doing it right the first time. You'll learn what "hardy" and "hardiness" really means in terms of plant selection and wintering over different plants.

This book is intended for folks who are not afraid of a challenge. Over and over I've heard people say you can't grow this and that in this harsh climate; yet I, and many others, have grown everything from acorn squash and sugar baby watermelon to azaleas and rhododendrons. It's not luck. It takes a little perseverance and learning a few secrets from fellow north country gardeners.

Happy gardening.

THE FIRST GARDENS

The first gardeners in the region were the Anishnabe, or "first people." The Indian women were the gardeners in most of the tribes across North America. They domesticated some of the plants which led to the practice of modern agriculture. For example, Indians cross-bred corn with wild grasses to develop hybrids which were suitable to different climates and growing conditions. Today, 60% of the food eaten around the world was developed by American Indians.

The American Indian method of gardening may seem odd by today's standards. However, it made sense in those days and also appealed to the spirits.

Ed Pine, a Chippewa Indian who lives on Sugar Island in Michigan's Upper Peninsula, remembers the old ways of his people. He remembers how they saved the seeds from radishes, corn and carrots to replant each year. Today, we call the seeds of these non-hybrids heirloom or traditional. Back then, it was survival. It was absolutely necessary to save seeds to plant the following year.

"They (his family and tribe) would just about starve before they would eat all of the dried corn from the previous summer," Pine recalled.

The Indians also knew how to cope with the short growing seasons in the North Country. They would plant vegetables early by sowing them deep into the soil. By the time the plant would appear above the ground the danger of frost was past and the plants would be well established.

Pine said shortly after the "Sugar Bush" or the tapping of trees for maple sugar, they would begin planting vegetables. It was about this time the suckers would start to run in a nearby creek. The Chippewas would catch the fish by hand and "plant" them under hills of corn as an offering to the spirit. Today, we know it was the nitrogen in the fish that gave the corn a boost.

Anything that grew above the ground was planted during the full moon, according to Pine. Underground vegetables were planted on the downside of the moon. American Indians didn't worry about weeding; they were too busy fishing the rapids area of the St. Mary's River which is now the Soo Locks. Pine said they didn't use livestock manure back then. They believed using animal excrement would cause sickness. They may not have known at the time, but by not fertilizing with animal manure they kept the weeds to a minimum.

In the fall, the Chippewas living on Sugar Island would make an offering of tobacco to the spirits for providing them with a bounty of potatoes, corn, pumpkin and other vegetables. Even today, Pine's grandsons, who have carried on the sugar bush tradition on the island, give an offering of tobacco to the gods after the sugar bush season is over.

How it All Began

The American Indian diet up until about the last 1000 years consisted mostly of meat and fish. Historians believe they also ate nuts and berries foraged in the wild. It was the South American Indians, and those who lived in the Southwestern United States, such as the Pueblos, who domesticated the vegetables common to our plates and palates. These vegetable seeds gradually found their way northward and eastward to the Chippewa, Ojibwa, Iroquoian and other Great Lakes Indians—and eventually to the white settlers.

Evidence suggests the Peruvian Indians of South America cultivated beans, gourds, cotton, squash, chili peppers, potatoes, tomatoes and other plants about 2300 B.C., long before the period that is commonly regarded as the beginning of modern agriculture. The gourds were hollowed out and used for containers or rattles for ceremonial purposes. However, archeologists have discovered nothing to indicate Eastern or Great Lakes Indians cultivated vegetables during this same period.

A few hundred years before Columbus' arrival in North America northern Indian tribes began using cultivation methods which led to what we regard as modern agriculture. The women planted the "three sisters"—squash, beans and

North Country Gardening

by Neil Moran

corn—and tended to their small garden plots using tools fashioned out of animal bones, saplings and rock. Some tribes, such as the Ioways, believed the spirit of young vegetables would be harmed by the men, thus the women were in charge of the planting, drying and storing of vegetables. They also chose certain women they believed to be "lucky" to drop the seed in the furrows. This, they hoped, would ensure a bountiful harvest.

Peppers, potatoes and tomatoes reached the American Indian population after 1492, via Spain. Tomatoes have historically been regarded as an ornamental plant; in fact, Thomas Jefferson and the

These Chippewa Indians are harvesting Manitok wild rice in Callaway, Minnesota.

early colonists grew tomatoes for their floral gardens only. The indians obviously knew a good thing when they tasted it!

The gardens of the northern tribes were small and appeared weedy by today's standards. Perhaps this was due to the types of plants Indians cultivated. For instance, maygrass, little barley, erect knotweed, amaranth and ragweed were grown for their starchy seeds, while purslane and carpet grass were grown for their tender edible leaves. These plants were never domesticated.

Zizania palustrus, or wild rice, was very popular with Great Lakes tribes, particularly the Algonquin. Tradition has it that in the early fall, the Chippewa families would set up camp near the wild rice fields and prepare for harvest. The men would pole their canoes through the rice paddies while the women would brush the rice into the canoe with sticks called "knockers." The rice was then brought to

shore and dried over an open fire. The outer shells were removed by walking on them in a skin-lined pit.

A celebration would then take place after the harvest giving thanks to Manitok, or the gods. The rice was often prepared and eaten during this ritual and then stored in mancocks (birchbark containers) until they were needed later.

Wild rice is still quite popular with Indians. Folks who travel along U.S. 2 and M-28 in the western Upper Peninsula of Michigan and into Wisconsin and Minnesota, will have several opportunities to purchase wild rice. Some, but not all, of this rice is grown by American Indians. Wild rice is rich in carbohydrates, low in fat and contains protein, thiamin, riboflavin and Vitamin B. It is much more nutritious than the cultivated grains introduced to North America such as barley, oats, wheat and rye. More importantly, it tastes great! It can be served as a side dish with meat, fish and vegetable entrees.

The Chippewa Indians harvest wild rice by the truckload on the White Earth Indian Reservation in Callaway, Minnesota. Folks can order wild rice directly from Manitok Wild Rice (see "Sources for Seeds and Equipment").

American Indian Vegetables

Browsing through seed catalogs one can readily spot vegetable seeds with indian sounding names such as Crookneck squash, Hopi blue corn and Aztec half runner beans. Many of these varieties were probably domesticated in South America and may not do so well in the North. However, several varieties are worth a try, including scarlet runner beans, Hopi lima beans and many types of edible and ornamental corn. Jerusalem artichokes and sunflowers were also domesticated by American Indians, the latter, of course, being quite suitable to this region.

SOURCES

How Indians Use Wild Plants For Food, Medicine & Crafts, by Francis Densmore, Dover Publications, 180 Varick St. NY., N.Y.

American Indians: An Illustrated History, introduction by Alvin M. Josephy Jr., Turner Publication Co., Atlanta Georgia.

OUR COLD CLIMATE

"Here is where winter spends its summers"

—anonymous

Prior to the summer of 1992 it had been a rule of thumb that here in the Eastern Upper Peninsula of Michigan we were safe from the dangers of frost after June 15th. Rules were meant to be broken, I guess. The last recorded frost that year was July 4th. Of course, it could have been worse: the Lower Peninsula town of Alpena reported seeing snow that morning!

My gardening neighbors generally agree that frost usually doesn't visit our gardens any later than the 15th of June. The **earliest** we'll see "frosts on the pumpkins" (or in many cases pumpkin vines) is about August 28. Of course, rules were meant to be broken, especially when predicting the weather in this harsh climate that is punctuated by mountains and surrounded by water.

And of course, this can vary from one northern hamlet to another. For instance, Washington Island, at the northern tip of Wisconsin's Door Peninsula, has an average frost-free season of 153 days—in contrast, the village of Watersmeet, in the western Upper Peninsula of Michigan, has only 65 frost-free days! This variation has a lot to do with lake effect. While cool breezes off the lake delay spring planting (especially along Lake Superior), its warming effect will delay late summer frosts by up to three weeks, in comparison to inland areas.

Experienced gardeners in the northern states fall into a groove of knowing what to expect, and plan accordingly. A string of nice days in mid-May is just that. It can easily be followed by several frosts and "unseasonably cold" weather. Thus, old timers in these regions are patient and watch the calendar rather than the weather.

This woman is selling cherries at a roadside stand near Traverse City Michigan. Cherries grow well in this "micro climate" along the shores of Lake Michigan.

In my locale I feel safest planting sweet corn by the first day of June, providing the weather is fairly warm for good germination. I know that if we do get a frost in the middle of June the corn will survive, unless it's a particularly severe frost and then I cover my seedlings with a little straw or hay. I also realize that I will need at least 75 good growing days (from germination to picking) and don't want to chance planting any later. Like one old timer related, "if you don't lose some plants to the elements, you're planting too late."

Hardiness maps

Caution is in order when examining "hardiness zone" maps in seed catalogs and the like. Apparently, someone is in a hurry when they create these. If taken literally, Sault Ste. Marie, Michigan (a place some folks call Sault Ste. Siberia) would be in the same hardiness zone as Detroit, Michigan, 300 miles to the south!

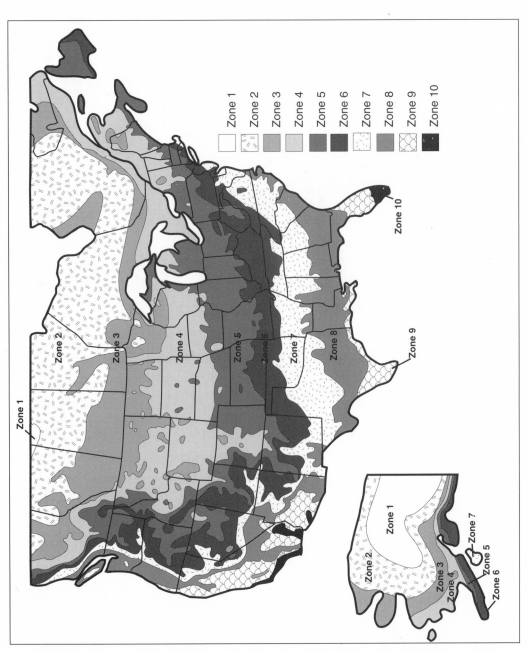

*Hardiness Zone Map (Developed from information from USDA). This map is a fairly accurate depiction of hardiness zones for northern areas. To be on the safe side, you can choose plants rated to one zone **below** the zone indicated for your area.*

Another problem with hardiness maps is it's virtually impossible to accurately plot all regions due to a variety of factors that affect climate such as proximity to lakes, mountains and ridges. For instance, someone living in an area designated "zone 4" on most hardiness maps may be misled if they live in a low lying area between ridges or mountains. Cool air tends to sink into these basins. In contrast, folks occupying high ground with a south facing slope near warm water may exceed a recommended hardiness zone.

I believe the USDA hardiness zone map provided in this section offers a fairly accurate picture of planting zones in the North, and the entire U.S. for that matter. Identifying your hardiness zone will save you time and money by ensuring you select varieties appropriate for your region. However, just to be on the safe side, I usually choose plants that are rated one zone below our hardiness zone. For example, although Sault Ste. Marie may fall into zone 4 on most maps, I try to select plants (flowers, shrubs etc.) that are rated to zone 3.

Rain! Rain! Rain!

You can also plan on it being wet in most northern locations. This can be a boon or a bust. Extended periods of cool rains in June can cause seeds and bulbs to germinate poorly. Thus, we try different tricks such as planting in hills or mounds, raised beds and trenching. And we try to be patient enough to wait just a little longer to plant our cold sensitive vegetables such as cucumbers and summer squash. One advantage we appear to have over our southern neighbors when it comes to rain is when it does rain it's more often a gentle shower compared to the terrible thunderstorms, hail and high winds common in the southern parts of states like Vermont and Maine.

Have I convinced you to turn in your hoe for galoshes and a wet suit? There's good news. By mid to late July when our southern neighbors are crying "it's too hot and dry," it's still relatively cool and moist in our region. Consequently, many vegetables are flourishing in our gardens such as potatoes, carrots and rutabagas. And our short season corn and pumpkin seeds we bought may not be doing too badly either.

North Country Gardening

by Neil Moran

Hardiness Rating Not Everything

Many seed and nursery catalogs rate plants according to hardiness. For example, an apple tree may be rated as "hardy to -30 degrees." Taken literally, this would mean that a plant will survive the winter as long as the mercury doesn't dip below -30 degrees. As you perhaps remember from the winter of (pick **your** year) 93-94, many shrubs, trees, roses and other plants rated hardy for the area didn't make it, even though they had survived some severe winters heretofore.

According to Steve Gregory, a Michigan State University horticulturist, hardiness rating is only part of the equation. How well a plant does during the growing season also plays a major role. In other words, it's important that a plant has a good year if it is to survive our winters. Thus, during the growing season, be sure to properly water, fertilize and mulch your plants if you want them to make it through the winter. Even then there's no guarantee they will survive, as the winter of 93-94 so aptly proved.

If you don't want to rely on hardiness labels or maps, experiment. It won't take long to determine that a fruit tree or exotic flower is out of its zone! Also, keep careful notes in a journal or diary of the first and last frosts and what did well or poorly each year. You will learn more from experience than you will relying on hardiness maps and labels on plants, which are after all, approximations at best.

And lo and behold, many trees, shrubs and other plants survive the "hardiness test" only to succumb to other disasters, such as being munched on by a deer or run over by a snowmobile. Take the advice of one northern gardener: plant three trees, one for yourself, one for the deer and one for the elements.

REFERENCES

The North Woods of Michigan, Wisconsin, Minnesota and Southern Ontario by Glenda Daniel and Jerry Sullivan, SIERRA CLUB BOOKS, SAN FRANCISCO

—Michigan State University, Upper Peninsula Experiment Station, Chatham Michigan

EEDS FOR THE NORTH

As you gaze across the white expanse of snow blanketing your garden, your thoughts invariably revert back to the pleasures you experienced in your garden the previous summer. You shake your head slowly, thinking of the long winter that lies ahead, then proceed to the mailbox and reach for the mail. As you dust the snow off the magazines, belated Christmas cards and bills you'd rather not look at—there they are.

The summer seed catalogs!

Page upon page of colorful flowers and vegetables stare back at you as the sky gets ready to dump another foot of snow.

But it doesn't matter. For the next few days you can let your mind wander across the pages and down the columns of tomatoes, carrots and sweet corn. For awhile you can forget about the snow stacked up just outside your door. For just one moment you can dream of wiping sweat off your brow as you reach down and pick a red ripe tomato.

Choosing a Seed Company

There are more seed catalogs out there than aphids on a cabbage. Just as you need to be choosy about seeds, you need to be choosy about seed catalogs. However, it's easy to select good seed catalogs; simply stick to nursery companies that test their products in the northern states and/or sell varieties suitable for this region.

There are a few things to be aware of when ordering from seed catalogs. For instance, pay attention to "days to maturity" for each vegetable. This actually means "good growing days" to ripen, or mature. For example, the corn I grow

North Country Gardening

by Neil Moran

Vegetable	Amount required per person	Spacing between rows	Spacing within rows	Planting depth	# of Days to germinate	# of Days to harvest time	Comments
Asparagus	12 crowns	24-36 in	12-18 in	6-8 in	Appears in 2-3 weeks	1-2 years	Hardy perennial; keep weeded and mulched.
Beans (wax & green)	1/4 lb	18-24 in	3-6 in	1 in	6-14 days	65-85	Prolific; avoid cultivating when wet.
Beans (lima)	1/4 lb	18 in	3-6 in	1 in	6-14 Days	90-110	Difficult to grow in North; try Fordhook variety.
Beets	1/2 pkt	18 in	4-8 in	1/2 in	8-12 days	50-65	Easy to grow; stores well.
Broccoli	2-3 plants	18 in	8-10 in	1/4 in	6-10 Days	60-80	Nutritious, prolific; grows well into fall.
Brussels Sprouts	4-5 plants	18 in	12-18 in	1/4 in	6-9 days	75-95	Grows huge plant; watch for insects.
Cabbage	5-6 plants	18 in	12-18 in	1/4 in	6-9	65-80	Keep dusted; generally grows well in North.
Carrots	1/2 pkt	18 in	3-5 in	1/4 in	12-18	60-85	Reliable; lots of varieties to choose from.
Cauliflower	4-5 plants	18 in	12-18 in	1/4 in	8-10	70-85	Grown from transplants or directly seeded in garden.
Cucumber	1 hill	24-48 in		1 in	7-10	60-85	Plant when weather is warm and settled.
Celery	4-6 plants	18 in	6-10 in	transplants	10-20	90-110	Grown up here from transplants only.
Cantaloupe	1 hill	24-36 in		1 in	9-15	75-100	Give it a try; Choose from short season varieties.
Corn	1/2 lbs	18-24 in	6-8 in	1 in	6-12	55-80	Raccoons love it! Many short season varieties to choose from.
Garlic	5 bulbs	24 in	4 in	2 in		90	Lots of health claims; grows well in North.
Lettuce	1/2 pkt	12-18 in	3-4 in	1/4 in	7-12	40-60	Choose a variety that's slow to bolt.

G U I D E   T O   P L A N T I N G   V E G E T A B L E S

Vegetable	Amount required per person	Spacing between rows	Spacing within rows	Planting depth	# of Days to germinate	# of Days to harvest time	Comments
Onions	6-10 bulbs	18 in	3-4 in	1-2 in	7-12	40-80	Grow well from bulbs; keep cultivated.
Parsnips	1/4 pkt	18 in	3-4 in	1/4 in	14-20	100-120	Wait until after frost to harvest.
Peas	1/2 lb	18 in	3-4 in	1 in	6-10	50-80	Thrive in cool, wet climate.
Peppers	1 plant	18 in	18 in	1/2 in	use plants	80-100	Heat loving plant that may benefit from a "season extender."
Potato	5-10 lb	18-24 in	10-24 in	3-4 in	12-18	60-100	The "tomato of the North." Grows well in sandy loam soil.
Pumpkin	1 hill	36-48 in		1 in	7-14	90-110	Bush varieties are best for mid-sized jack-o-lanterns.
Radish	1/4 pkt	12-18 in	3-5 in	1/4 in	3-6	25-35	Grows well anywhere, anytime.
Rutabaga	1/4 pkt	18 in	6-10 in	1/4 in	5-10	90-100	Easy to grow; good with pasties and Thanksgiving dinner.
Squash (winter)	1 hill	36-48 in		1 in	7-10	85-110	Choose winter varieties carefully to ensure a harvest.
Squash (summer)	1 hill	36-48		1 in	7-10	60-80	One hill may be all you need; save space for other veggies.
Spinach	1/2 pkt	12-18 in	3-5 in	1/4 in	7-12	40-50	Loves cool climate; nutritious.
Tomato	2-3 plants	18-14 in	18 in	1/2 in	7-14	60-90	A challenge to northern gardeners; look for short season varieties.
Watermelon (icebox)	1 plant	24-36		1 in	7-12	80-110	With a little pampering, they can be grown in the North.

Suggested Planting Guide for Northern Gardeners

Mid to Late May	Memorial Day**—first week of June	Mid-June or after last frost
Carrots	Winter Squash	Lima Beans
Rutabagas	Corn	Snap Beans
Peas	Tomatoes	Beets
Beets	Cucumbers	Carrots
Onions	Summer Squash	Head Lettuce
Potatoes*	Dill	Radish
Asparagus	Late Peas	Spinach
Leaf Lettuce	Late Potatoes	Kohlrabi
Radish	Cantaloupe	
Turnips	Watermelons	
Parsley	Pumpkins	
Broccoli		
Spinach		

  * Protect from frost by covering with dirt or plastic

** Most of these crops (especially corn, melons, squash and pumpkin) must get in the ground early to have a chance of setting fruit before the growing season ends.

(Sunglow Hybrid Sweet Corn from Gurney's Seed & Nursery) requires 65-70 days to maturity. This means 65-70 days with daytime temperatures above 70 degrees or better are needed to grow an ear of sweet corn.

In general, choose vegetable varieties that require less than 70 days to maturity. However, I have grown other vegetables that required a whopping 85-90 days to maturity (such as squash and pumpkin) with a great deal of success. Unfortunately, you have do a great deal of fussing to get these varieties to mature by season's end.

However, for most vegetables it's neither necessary nor advisable to choose varieties that require over 70 growing days to ripen. Fortunately, there are many nursery companies, such as Johnny's Selected Seeds out of Maine, High Altitude Gardens in Iowa and even Gurney's in South Dakota, who offer varieties for short growing seasons. Thus, most years you can count on vine ripe vegetables, providing you've done a little homework and selected short-season varieties.

John Holm, who is a nurseryman, plant breeder and horticulturist in Fairbanks, Alaska, says you can't overestimate the importance of seed selection. He said most seed companies are in the business to sell seeds, thus it's important to select the right varieties from the right companies. He also said it's important to rely on your local nursery for seeds and plants and to listen to the advice of your neighbors.

Hardiness Zones

While perusing seed catalogs it's worth your while to pay attention to hardiness zones. Some of these can be misleading for the northern gardener. Hardiness zone maps in seed catalogs sometimes lack detail, thus a whole region may be lumped into an inappropriate zone. For instance, the Upper Peninsula of Michigan (zone 3-4) often gets lumped in the same zone as Detroit (zone 5-6), which is 300 miles to the south. The hardiness zone map in this book provides a more accurate labeling of your area.

Some catalogs offer a whole range of information about a seed variety by using picture codes. For instance, Johnny's Selected Seeds uses tiny pictures and abbreviations to indicate a variety's tolerance to cool weather; it will also indicate if it's an heirloom, hybrid or a specialty item. This information is quite helpful for folks like us who need specifics on what will grow in our particular locale.

A Few Words About Hybrids

Have you ever tried to save seeds to plant the following year only to find out they didn't do so well? Perhaps you planted a hybrid variety. Hybrids are genetically altered seeds which combine the attributes of two or more parent plants. When re-planting these seeds it's like shuffling a deck of cards—the cards representing genes; you really don't know what kind of hand the plant will be dealt.

North Country Gardening
by Neil Moran

This genetic engineering makes plants more adaptable to different climates and market needs. In the north, certain hybrids were developed (such as my favorite, Hybrid Sunglow Sweet Corn) which are suitable for our short growing seasons. Another desirable attribute that results from cross breeding is a plant's ability to bear numerous fruit on space saving vines, such as Autumn Gold bush variety pumpkins.

Heirloom and Traditional Seeds

Many northerners could be described as "traditional" in the sense they prefer the natural to the man-made, the home made to the store bought. And what the heck, we like to save money.

There's a quiet but significant movement to preserve traditional and heirloom vegetable and flower seeds. Our garden seeds date back at least 10,000 years, when human beings first decided to preserve a seed and replant it. Seeds are living history in the sense that they span from generation to generation and continent to continent. For instance, American Indians passed on heirloom seeds such as Hopi sweet corn and Aztec half runner beans the same way they did their folklore and legends. And today, with the fall of the Iron Curtain, Russians are trading their heirloom varieties with folks around the world.

Unfortunately, according to some scientists, we're loosing many heirloom varieties so rich in history. Approximately 27,000 plant species are becoming extinct each year as modern agriculture relies on a handful of species for gardening and farming. There is one group which aims to curtail this rapid extinction of plants. The Seed Savers Exchange is part of a larger movement to preserve, as has been done for thousands of years, unique species of open-pollinated and traditional seeds. Another group with similar goals is called Seeds of Change, out of Santa Fe, New Mexico. Both of these groups offer heirloom and traditional seeds for folks who are concerned with preserving our natural plant heritage.

When deciding whether to plant traditional or heirloom varieties, seed selection becomes even more critical for the cold climate gardener due to the fact many open-pollinated varieties and heirlooms don't perform so well in the North. Of

course, that's why they've been cross-pollinated as hybrids. Thus, the green thumb will have to do a little digging to locate open-pollinated varieties suitable for this region.

The best bet for success with open-pollinated varieties in the northern region, at least for the beginning seed collector, are cool weather vegetables. Many varieties, in fact, have never been cross-pollinated and do well in cool season climates including snap beans, English peas, lettuce, leeks, radishes and many different herbs. Open pollinated flowers suitable for the northern regions include French marigold, nasturtium, phlox, cosmos, dahlia, alyssum, balsam, calendula and celosia.

Robert L. Johnson, founder and chairman of Johnny's Selected Seeds, harvests leeks on one of their many test plots in Albion, Maine.

Beets, cabbage, carrots, cauliflower, cucumber, eggplant, onion, peppers, pumpkin, spinach, summer and winter squash, sweet corn, tomatoes and watermelons are available in both standard and hybrid varieties.

Garden City Seeds out of Victor, Montana, offers heirloom varieties worth experimenting with here in the north including Camberley and Danvers Half Long carrots (requires 75 days to maturity), Art Verrels sweet corn, (70 days), Black Seeded Simpson (42 days), Salad Bowl lettuce (46 days), Alderman peas (70-75 days) and Burbank Russet white potato.

High Altitudes Gardens deals exclusively with heirloom and organic varieties suitable for the North. In fact, these folks made a trip to Siberia in 1989 and brought back varieties they thought would be suitable to grow in mountainous regions. Some of these **should** grow in our backyards!

Galina's, Perestroika, Peasant and Glasnost are a few of the tomato varieties the folks from High Altitudes brought home with them. I've found these varieties germinate well and produce a strong stemmed plant. These imports will produce ripe tomatoes quicker than most varieties common in the U.S. However, some folks complain that they are not as tasty as Uncle Sam's tomatoes; you be the judge!

Saving Seeds

When I think of saving seeds I think of when, as kids, we would scoop out a handful of seeds out of the inside of a Jack-o-Lantern and tuck away but never get around to planting the following year.

There's a little more to saving seeds than drying and storing a few seeds until the following year. However, it need not be that complicated and can certainly lead to hours of enjoyment. Serious seed savers don't neglect to plant their seeds the following year.

The hybrids I mentioned earlier aren't suitable for saving due to the fact they won't reproduce true to form. Also, you need to be aware of self-pollinating varieties in contrast to those that rely on insects to pollinate.

Tomatoes are self-pollinating. These plants don't allow pollination by insects; thus, if you want seeds to save from tomatoes and other self-pollinating plants you can plant as many varieties as you want without worrying about cross-pollination.

In contrast, corn, squash and sunflower rely on insects for pollination. To avoid the possibility of cross-pollination of two or more different varieties of the same plant, space your planting times so they don't flower at the same time.

Carrots, lettuce and turnips may be either self pollinating or open pollinating. These are also biennials, meaning they produce seed the second year they're in the ground. Make sure these varieties don't cross with other species, even those living in the wild such as chantenay carrots crossing with Queen Anne's Lace or iceberg lettuce crossing with a wild lettuce.

The northern gardener can take advantage of seed saving to identify and collect tried and true varieties most likely to succeed year after year here in the

North. With our short growing seasons it's important to identify vegetable types which will produce in our harsh climate.

Saving seeds is really quite simple, once you've identified the self pollinating, non-self pollinating and hybrid varieties. At the end of each season, let the plants go to seed, then pick and dry them gradually (not in full sun or heat such as an oven) by hanging the plants up or spreading them out in a dry place. When the seeds are completely dry, store in Mason jars or a similar air tight container, in a cool, dry, dark place.

Saving seeds is a hobby within a hobby. It's another way we can enjoy gardening. Selecting hybrid and/or traditional seeds suitable for this region will give us something to do while the sun gradually melts the three feet of snow covering your garden.

REFERENCES

—*Seed Savers Exchange: Passing On Our Vegetable Heritage*, 3076 North Winn Rd. Decorah, Iowa 52101

—*Going Hybrid*, Michigan Country Lines, Jan/Feb 1994

—*Seed Savers Alert: Plan Now To Save Later!* By Suzanne Ashworth, Organic Gardening, March 1992.

—*Seeds of Change*, 1364 Rufina Circle #5, Santa Fe New Mexico 87501.

—*Down to Earth Vegetable Gardening Know-How*, Dick Raymond, Garden Way Publishing, 1975.

SOIL: *Foundation for a Successful Garden*

The northern region has unique soil and geological traits. It's a soil scientist's dream to have the chance to study the different soil types in our region; for instance, the Vilas loamy sand of Northern Wisconsin and the loamy silt clay in Ontonagon Michigan. And the geologist has a ball studying the sandstone and granite cliffs of Maine and Vermont!

For the gardener, it can be pure hell. Folks in predominantly clay regions have to cope with soil that won't dry up—or warm up—in the spring. In contrast, folks near the lakes or otherwise sandy locations, crave the rich black dirt needed to grow luscious flowers and vegetables.

Making Soil Gardener Friendly

Fortunately, there are several ways we can improve our garden soil (without needing a soil scientist or geologist).

First, examine the nature of the soil. Is it predominantly sandy, clay or a sandy loam? The latter is the best soil for growing vegetables. One will readily notice its black nutrient-rich appearance and slightly sandy quality which helps the ground "breathe" while still retaining water and nutrients.

On the other hand, a purely sandy soil can be a problem. Sand is made up of tiny stony particles which allow soil aeration. Sandy soil does not hold water well. Add organic matter to sandy soil, such as well rotted manure, grass clippings and compost. The organic matter—or humus—will help bring these diminutive particles together and take on a sponge-like quality. The results are better moisture and nutrient retention.

For heavy clay soils, again add organic matter. When added to clay, the humus will break up the clay-forming particles which will allow moisture and air to seep through while still retaining nutrients.

Generally speaking, organic matter cannot be added all at once to improve a sandy or heavy clay soil. The best way is to add compost and manure at the beginning of the season, work it under, then repeat in the fall. This is a good practice to continue even after you've initially improved the soil.

The second consideration is the nutrient content of the soil. This is achieved with a soil test. Soil test kits can be purchased from seed catalogs for as little as $15. Or, you can send your sample to a county extension agent; they'll do it for less than what it would cost to buy a kit. For the home gardener you should test your soil about every five years, unless your soil is extremely poor and you want to monitor its progress on an annual basis.

The major nutrients measured by soil tests are nitrogen, phosphorus, and potassium. If a soil test finds any of these nutrients to be lacking, organic or inorganic fertilizers should be added to the soil. Inorganic fertilizers offer the easiest and quickest method of adding these nutrients. A fertilizer labeled 12-12-12, for instance, means it contains 12% of each of the three major nutrients. A fertilizer labeled 25-25-25 is, of course, much more potent. Caution is in order here, however. Plants that receive, for example, too much nitrogen will produce a lot of vine or foliage, but bear little fruit; try to avoid too much of a good thing.

Inorganic fertilizers are applied at a rate of ten pounds per 1000 square feet of garden soil. Nurseries usually sell fertilizer in ten pound bags. Local feed stores sell fertilizer cheaper in 50 pounds bags and up. A fifty pound bag of fertilizer is enough to do a fairly large garden and still have enough left to side-dress plants later in the season.

If you shudder at the thought of adding inorganic products to your garden, you're not alone. Many people are turning to organic fertilizers to get the nutrients plants need. One advantage of organic fertilizers, such as compost and manure, is they contribute to the composition of your soil. In contrast, inorganic fertilizers release nutrients for the plants to use then literally disappear into the air.

by Neil Moran

Well rotted sheep, chicken, cow manure and compost are the best sources of plant nutrients, including nitrogen. Organic additives will do more to improve your soil in the long run than will inorganic fertilizer. If you can swing a deal with a local farmer, manure is also the cheapest way to fertilize your garden. A pick-up truckload of well rotted manure is sufficient to do a 30 ft. X 30 ft. garden.

I compromise and use both inorganic and organic fertilizers. If you have good garden soil you won't need to feed all of your plants inorganic fertilizers. I reserve granular fertilizers for my corn, squash, pumpkin and tomatoes, even then using them sparingly.

Don't forget the flower beds. Years of growing bulbs and perennials in the same location will seriously deplete beds and borders of necessary nutrients. Adding manure and compost is the best way

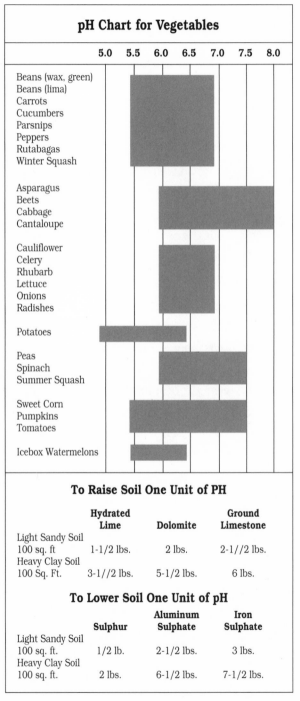

pH Chart for Vegetables

| | 5.0 | 5.5 | 6.0 | 6.5 | 7.0 | 7.5 | 8.0 |

Beans (wax, green), Beans (lima), Carrots, Cucumbers, Parsnips, Peppers, Rutabagas, Winter Squash

Asparagus, Beets, Cabbage, Cantaloupe

Cauliflower, Celery, Rhubarb, Lettuce, Onions, Radishes

Potatoes

Peas, Spinach, Summer Squash

Sweet Corn, Pumpkins, Tomatoes

Icebox Watermelons

To Raise Soil One Unit of PH

	Hydrated Lime	Dolomite	Ground Limestone
Light Sandy Soil 100 sq. ft	1-1/2 lbs.	2 lbs.	2-1//2 lbs.
Heavy Clay Soil 100 Sq. Ft.	3-1//2 lbs.	5-1/2 lbs.	6 lbs.

To Lower Soil One Unit of pH

	Sulphur	Aluminum Sulphate	Iron Sulphate
Light Sandy Soil 100 sq. ft.	1/2 lb.	2-1/2 lbs.	3 lbs.
Heavy Clay Soil 100 sq. ft.	2 lbs.	6-1/2 lbs.	7-1/2 lbs.

Composition Breakdown of Organic Matter			
Material	**Nitrogen**	**Phosphoric Acid (P)**	**Potash (K)**
Mulches			
Alfalfa hay	2.5	.5	2.0
Grain straw	.6	.2	1.0
Peat	2.3	.4	.8
Sawdust	.2	—	—
Timothy hay	1.0	.2	1.5
Barnyard Manures			
Cow manure	1.3	.9	.8
Chicken manure	2.8	2.8	1.5
Horse manure, fresh	.6	.3	.5
Pig manure, fresh	.6	.5	.4
Sheep manure	1.4	1.0	3.0
Other Organics			
Bonemeal	2.0	22.0	—
Cottonseed meal	6.0	3.0	1.0
Dried blood meal	13.0	1.5	.8
Fish meal	10.0	6.0	—
Fish scrap	5.0	3.0	—
Sewerage sludge	2.0	1.4	.8
Soybean meal	7.0	1.2	1.5
Wood ashes	—	1.8	5.0

to improve and maintain the soil in your flower beds. Apply gradually over an extended period of time.

The pH Test

A soil tester will also test the pH level in the soil. A productive garden will have a soil which is neither too acidic nor too alkaline. It is important that soil has a balanced pH to be capable of utilizing nutrients present in the soil. Balanced pH is between 6.3 and 7.

Some vegetables and fruits prefer a slightly acidic soil. Acid loving plants include potatoes, blueberries, lupine and primrose. Acid soil has a pH range between 5.8 and 6. Some folks leave a portion of their garden acidic (don't apply any lime to this section) to grow acid loving plants.

Sweeten acidic soil with lime. Spread a 12 quart bucket of lime to every 1000 square feet of garden soil. Do this every three or four years to maintain the proper pH range. Wood ashes from a wood stove can be used as a substitute for lime, only double the dose by applying two 12 quart buckets (instead of one) to every 1000 square feet of soil.

Soil pH is lowered with an application of sulphur. One half pound of sulphur per 100 square feet of garden space will lower the pH by one unit.

Old garden plots and flower beds can be revived with an application of lime and several applications of organic matter (compost, manure etc.). A soil test will

tell you if your garden is lacking nutrients (yellow leaves on corn and other plants is another tell tale sign).

There are other ways to renew an old garden, including planting cover crops, such as rye and buckwheat. This is a good way of practicing crop rotation while adding organic matter to the soil (see section on cover crops). Crop rotation is important to maintain healthy, fertile soil. Or you could do like I did one unseasonably cold summer; I didn't plant anything. Instead, I spent the summer working lime, compost and well rotted sheep manure into the soil. The following year I had one of the best gardens I've had in years.

So before your garden becomes a field trip for university students, set aside time to improve the soil. Then step back and watch it grow!

REFERENCES

—*Down to Earth Vegetable Gardening Know-How*, Dick Raymond, Garden Way Publishing, 1975.

TARTING FROM SEED

Starting plants indoors or in a greenhouse is a good way to extend the growing season in the short season zones. And it may be just what the doctor ordered—you can find relief for the winter blahs by seeing new growth sprout up before the snow has actually melted outside.

February is a good time to go over the multitude of colorful offerings in the seed catalogs. By the end of the month you will be ready to order a few seeds to start inside. If you haven't found a good seed source for northern climates, ask around, or refer to the list of seed sources at the back of this book.

Starting Seeds: The Basics

Light, heat and moisture are basic ingredients to take into consideration when starting plants indoors. Unfortunately, we can't rely on sunny days in the spring in this country to provide adequate lighting to get plants started. So we must resort to artificial lighting.

But first we must germinate the seed.

Veteran North country gardeners Janice and Jerry Kessler, who live along the St. Mary's River near Sault Ste. Marie, Michigan, start their seeds in late March and early April. They use 2" deep wooden flats placed on top of the protective sheet metal liner on their wood stove. The moderate heat of the wood stove heats the seed starting medium to 75-80 degrees. A thermometer is used to monitor the temperature of their starting mix.

The Kesslers germinate the seed in a sterile non-soil mixture of vermiculite, sphagnum peat moss, fertilizer and other nutrients called "Promix" (this, or a similar germinating mix can be purchased at your local garden center). This mixture is

Shonna and Ric Vernagus, owners of Magilla's Greenhouse, start all their own plants from seed in the greenhouse Ric built in Pickford Michigan.

dampened thoroughly prior to planting. The seed is then sown, according to instructions on the packet, and covered with wet paper toweling and Saran Wrap to keep in the moisture. The Kesslers keep their seed flats damp by watering them each day with a mist spray bottle.

In three to four days the Kesslers have sprouted seeds (note: some seeds may take longer to germinate and will need light; refer to instructions on individual seed packets).

Now comes light (in addition to daily watering of the newly germinated seed). According to Shonna Vernagus, proprietor of Magilla's Greenhouse in Pickford, Michigan, light is the most important element for starting transplants. I've learned from experience that relying on the light from the northern sun to start transplants isn't enough. In fact, I've set seedlings in a south facing window of the house only to be disappointed when I watch the plants become long and leggy as they reach for scarce, but precious, light; thus, you'll need artificial lighting.

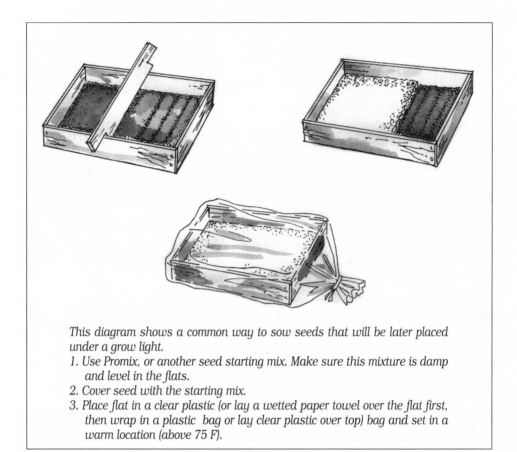

This diagram shows a common way to sow seeds that will be later placed under a grow light.
1. *Use Promix, or another seed starting mix. Make sure this mixture is damp and level in the flats.*
2. *Cover seed with the starting mix.*
3. *Place flat in a clear plastic (or lay a wetted paper towel over the flat first, then wrap in a plastic bag or lay clear plastic over top) bag and set in a warm location (above 75 F).*

The cheapest way to provide artificial lighting is with a fluorescent shop light. A 50 inch fluorescent light and a couple of 48 inch bulbs can be purchased for less than $15 at a retail store. These lights need to be suspended within 2-3 inches of your seedlings for optimal benefit. They can be left on for up to 16 hours each day. Or you can purchase a Halite for a couple hundred dollars. This unit will provide higher intensity lighting and can be suspended 1-2 feet above the seedlings. Regardless of which unit you use, you'll need an automatic timer for convenience and consistent lighting.

When the seedlings develop their second or third set of leaves, transplant to a slightly deeper container. These new containers should be sterilized by washing them with a mixture of one part bleach to nine parts water, according to Vernagus.

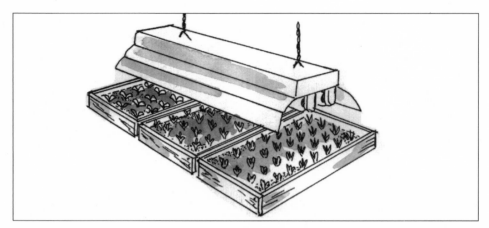

A grow light is indispensable for starting plants in the North. Suspend the light as close to the plants as possible. Use a timer to allow at least 16 hours of light per day. Grow lights produce, stocky, compact plants which will be ready to take on the elements.

It is common practice to remove the plants from the original containers by taking hold of the leaves rather than the stems. Use a popsicle stick to loosen the roots.

The seedlings can now be placed under the grow light. Be sure to water them each day. I spray mine with lukewarm water each morning before I go to work, then again in the evening. Also, try to keep the room temperature around 70 degrees during the day and between 60 and 65 degrees at night.

If you don't want to go to the expense and trouble of acquiring a greenhouse, you can simply leave your plants under a grow light until it's time to harden them off outside. A 50 inch long grow light and container will allow you

When the plants form 2-3 leaves remove them from your planting flats by loosening the soil around them first with a Popsicle stick. Then gently pull out the plant by the leaves.

Jerry Kessler inside his quonset style greenhouse he built for under $50 with conduit pipe, plywood and plastic sheeting.

to start all your tomatoes, peppers and a few flowers. When these get big and healthy you can move them to a sunny window to make room for quick starting plants such as cabbage, broccoli and marigolds.

Moving Plants Outdoors

If you move your seedlings to a greenhouse, think heat. A small greenhouse can be extended from a bedroom or living room window, taking advantage of the heat from your home. If your greenhouse is an extension of an outbuilding or is free standing, acquire a small electric thermostatically controlled heater. A "hot scot," which is similar to a hot plate, will provide adequate heat for a small (less than 50 square feet) area. A small ceramic fan with a blower is also a good choice; the fan will distribute heat to the corners of the greenhouse.

Greenhouses come in all shapes and sizes. I discourage folks from ordering expensive greenhouses advertised in garden magazines and seed catalogs. The high winds and heavy snows in this country make this a risky and expensive venture. If you **do** decide to purchase a greenhouse—and there are many quality ones out there—you may wish to consider disassembling the unit and storing it during the winter.

After some healthy trial and error, Jerry Kessler constructed a portable greenhouse for under $50. He uses 2 X 4's, plywood and conduit pipe to build a quonset type frame. He drapes a ten foot sheet of plastic polyethylene sheeting over the frame. For a heat source Jerry uses a small fan-forced heater placed on the floor inside. He assembles his quonset greenhouse in an area in his yard that is partially protected from the northwest winds, or "Alberta Clippers" which are legendary in this country. Jerry sets his up each year as soon as the snow has left his yard.

Daytime temperatures in a greenhouse should average around 70 degrees—about 60 degrees at night. You should also plan to provide ventilation. This can be accomplished by installing a small fan vented either through the plastic sheeting or the plywood walls.

Water your plants each day with a spray bottle or an inexpensive garden sprayer. Cool weather crops, such as cauliflower and broccoli, can be placed at the bottom of the greenhouse where it's cooler; tomatoes should be placed near the top.

Be careful! It's easy to burn young plants. Open up your greenhouse during hot weather to prevent overheating your plants. The Kesslers apply a light coating of yellow spray paint to the clear plastic to protect their fledgling plants from the sun's intense heat. On the other hand, close it up at night to protect your seedlings from those more-often-than-not cool spring evenings.

When your plants are well established and temperatures are climbing into the 60's and 70's, take them outdoors (if using an quonset type greenhouse, simply open up the doors and peel back the plastic sheeting). This is called hardening off. Set them in a shady spot at first, gradually moving them into the sun over the next few days. Make sure they're protected from the wind and heavy rains at this stage.

Greenhouse gardening can extend your growing season by several weeks. Quite frankly, starting your own transplants is probably not much cheaper than buying them from a supermarket or nursery (with the exception of perennials and herbs). However, you can grow healthier plants better suited to this area and receive a lot of satisfaction knowing you selected and grew the plants that will adorn your garden all summer.

EASON EXTENDERS: *Beat the Short Season!*

So how do we squeeze a few more days, weeks or even a month out of our growing season? I asked John Holm of Fairbanks, Alaska, who is a nurseryman and plant breeder, how he copes with the short seasons up there. He said there is only 90 days between frosts where he lives. And in addition he has to deal with the extended hours of daylight. To garden successfully he has had to do a great deal of selective breeding as well as gathering seeds and plants from all over the world.

Holm said he has an "established process" he goes through in order to garden successfully in Alaska. He uses a trial and error method but also takes advantage of special cultural practices. Some of these practices I call "season extenders." These include everything from covering plants with fabric row covers to providing wind protection for tomatoes.

Gardening Year-round

Actually, for the true garden lover, there are opportunities to garden year round. Begin the year by browsing through the seed catalogs that start arriving in January; start your seeds indoors in March and with a little luck you can start working the garden in late April. From May through September we do what we love best—tend to our fruits, vegetables and flowers. August and September is spent harvesting, canning, freezing and storing our produce. We can also enjoy some autumn gardening by tending to our flowers: the asters, purple coneflowers and other fall bloomers—covering them as needed to protect them from frost; yes, hoping to squeeze another week or two of beauty out of our beds and borders. At Thanksgiving and Christmas we enjoy the fruits of our labors, and the whole cycle starts over in January.

But how can we extend the time, for instance, squash has to mature on the vine? How can we squeeze a little more heat out of nature to allow our tomatoes to ripen? Finally, how can we turn 90 frost free days into 120? There are several answers to these questions.

However, first consider a planting strategy. Just like building a house or going fishing we need to make plans. In these parts especially, it's crucial to know what we're going to plant and when we're going to plant it.

Planting Strategies

Squash, pumpkin, watermelon and tomatoes simply must get started early to have a chance of maturing. Plant these as soon as the weather is reasonably mild (see culture for individual vegetables) and use row covers and hot caps to help them through the poor weather. Once they've made it through a couple of frosts and a wind storm they should be on their way!

One way to get a head start on your vine crops is to soak the seeds overnight or germinate them between sheets of paper towel. Either way, leave the seeds in a warm place (above 70 degrees) before planting.

Don't worry too much about the cool weather crops: carrots, rutabagas, peas, turnips and onions. These crops can take a frost just fine. In fact, start gardening outside early by planting these vegetables as soon as the soil can be worked. Corn is another one. Though not as frost tolerant as others, corn can tolerate a light frost both in the spring and late summer. I usually get my corn in no later than Memorial Day. If it comes up ahead of the last frost, I lay a protective cover of straw over the seedlings. Most years, I just leave it alone, if I'm not expecting a se-vere (less than 30 degrees) frost.

On the other hand, beans, cucumbers, and zucchini are quite sensitive to frost. Fortunately, these don't need to get in the the ground real early. Wait until all danger of frost is past before you plant. Or use row covers and hot caps to get these plants off to an early start, thus extending the season by a few days.

North Country Gardening

by Neil Moran

Hot Caps and Row Covers

Plant most of your crops as soon as the weather has settled, keeping in mind that it probably won't stay that way long. Prepare for some foul weather including the inevitable frost. Our weapons are row covers, hot caps, blankets, newspapers and water hoses. Keep these things close by so they can be activated at a moment's notice. In fact, I've had to deploy my arsenal of frost fighting equipment in the middle of the night!.

Hot caps can be constructed in various ways. These simple devices protect small plants from frost and help get plants, such as peppers, off to an early start.

Row covers are an excellent way to "jump start" your squash, pumpkins and other vegetables.

Hot caps and row covers are two "season extenders" that are worthy of the time spent fussing with them. Hot caps are like "mini greenhouses" which will raise the inside temperature between 5 and 15 degrees. They can be purchased from seed catalogs or fashioned out of milk cartons or 32 oz. soft drink bottles. Milk jugs and soda bottles can be cut off at the bottom to form a 6-8 inch high "hot cap." A triangle is cut away on one side to allow for ventilation. I've had considerable luck starting my peppers inside hot caps.

Row covers are another ingenious invention designed to aid us in

Glass cloches help Alan Alexander's tomatoes and peppers get off to a good start.

combating the cool days and nights in the North. Row covers can be purchased from seed catalogs and garden supply companies for about $8.00 (for a 64 in. by 25 ft. roll). These can be used to warm the ground for germination (I've had great success using them to get a head start on my squash and watermelon), to protect plants from frost or simply to get your favorite vegetable to ripen quicker. They also act as a shield against insects.

Glass Cloches

The English have used a season extending method for years to speed up their tomatoes, peppers and other cherished vegetables. They're called glass cloches which is a fancy English term for hinged window frames. Alan Alexander learned this method in his native England and brought his knowledge to Erin, Ontario, where he's lived and gardened for several years now.

Allan not only gets his hard-to-grow vegetables, such as tomatoes and peppers, off to a good start (and even better finish!) using glass cloches, but he has enviable early harvests of broccoli and lettuce using the cloche method. Alan can

use this method for either long (10-20 feet) rows of plants or to protect two or three plants, such as tomatoes and peppers.

Alan hinges his windows together, which is necessary to guard against the punishing effects of the wind. This method will involve an initial investment of time—and perhaps money—if you have to purchase windows. However, old storm windows are often listed for give away in the newspapers or radio buy-sell-or-trade programs. The busy north gardener (who may need time to fish on the side) may want to limit this method to a few of his or her more challenging vegetables such as tomatoes and peppers.

Tomato Extenders

Charlie and Kathy Nye, owners of Nye's Vegetable Farm in Hessel, Michigan, have used the wall-o-water method to extend the season with tomatoes. Charlie said a person can really get tomatoes off to a good start with this method. Plastic water-filled tubes surround the tomatoes. During the day the water in the tubes heats up; at night, the heat is released to the benefit of heat loving tomatoes. Wall-o-waters can be purchased from garden catalogs or at garden supply stores.

Jerry Kessler of Sault Ste. Marie isn't exactly sold on wall-o-waters. He and wife Janice, found these cumbersome to work with. Instead, they surround their

Starting plants in these wire cages surrounded by a garbage bag will get tomatoes off to a good start.

tomato plants with a 18-24 inch high garden fence (chicken wire, yard fence etc.), then slip a black garbage bag over it. The bottom is then cut out of the bag (which now becomes the top). This method will protect the young plants from the wind; it also conducts and retains much needed heat—all this for just pennies.

They let the plants grow inside these circular shelters until the tomatoes ripen—which lo and behold they usually do. Jerry shared this idea with me and I'm sure glad he did!

Here's another way to "extend" the season with tomatoes (I swear there are more tricks for coaxing tomatoes than any other vegetable). Simply surround three sides of the plant or plants with bales of straw. Lean an old window or plastic sheeting frame over the side that is open. Allow for ventilation. This will protect the young tomatoes from those awful winds and cool weather in late May and early June. However, don't leave it on should the weather warm up above 65 degrees.

Protection Against Frost

In late August, and especially into September, we start listening to the radio. Our ears perk up when we hear "danger of frost," especially if we live in "low lying areas." It's frustrating to a lot of northern growers when we get a frost in late August or early September, followed by several days or even weeks of nice weather before the next frost attacks our flower and vegetable gardens.

One way to protect against a late summer frost is to cover your flowers and vegetables with sheets and blankets. Frost, which is nothing more than cold air, descends downward from above the plants. Plants are naturally protected by the heat radiating from the soil, unless of course, we get a severe frost. Thus, we use blankets to smother the plants, drawing them closer to the warm soil. The problem with blankets is if they get wet from the dew overnight and become heavy the whole chore hardly seems worth it. You can avoid this frustration by removing the blankets the following morning and letting them hang to dry.

For a large garden, it may not be possible to save everything. That is why, each year, I try my best to have my huge, bushy squash and pumpkin plants bear ripe fruit before Jack Frost arrives.

North Country Gardening

by Neil Moran

These tomato plants are set out before the danger of frost is past. The coffee cans can be quickly mobilized to protect the plants from frost.

The most practical way to extend the growing season in the fall is to plant cool weather vegetables which grow right into fall without a worry about frost. Potatoes, carrots, onions, broccoli, Brussels sprouts and rutabagas can all give you a chance to garden right into October, which for this region is doing pretty good (southern gardeners talk about gardening past Christmas!). The big problem I have with fall gardening is the incessant rain which makes my garden (which is only a half mile from a large river) pretty soggy. Therefore, I've got to be careful not to leave my root crops in the ground too long.

Extend the Season with Mulches

Mulches are season extenders to some extent. They supply plants with extra nutrients while trapping in moisture. They also keep the ground warm at night. Mulches include anything from well rotted barnyard manure and grass clippings to old newspapers and black plastic. The nice thing about organic mulches is once you spread them on you don't have to worry about them again. In contrast, newspaper and black plastic has to be taken up in the fall, which can be a messy job.

The Nyes of Hessel, Michigan extend the season for melons by surrounding them with black plastic. The plastic draws in the heat this sweet fruit so badly craves. I use black plastic to surround my watermelons and cantaloupes to ripen them by season's end.

Raised Beds

Another way to extend the season, or have a more productive one, is to plant in raised beds. These are quite popular in the North; in fact, some folks garden exclusively with raised beds. Raised beds allow you to create your own soil medium. This type of gardening is popular with folks who must otherwise garden in clay or sand.

Raised beds can be constructed in your front yard by removing the topsoil or right in the middle of the garden. Raised beds are usually surrounded by treated lumber, old railroad ties or large stones to contain the soil. Within the beds you can add the soil and amendments you think are needed to grow what you want.

Raised beds amended with rich humus is a good way to cope with cool, heavy soil types.

Raised beds can increase the soil temperature 5-8 degrees, thus extending the season by providing richer, warmer soil for plants to take root. These beds also allow better drainage, especially critical in May and June in many areas. Raised beds are also advantageous due to the fact you can reach into the bed from each side to do your hoeing without compacting the soil with your feet. And lastly, old timers and disabled folks can sit on the timbers and pluck weeds from their gardens, something we all will have to consider some day!

Ken Biron, who lives on Sugar Island near Sault Ste. Marie, has had good luck with raised beds. He fills a tractor tire with dirt and sticks his tomato plants inside. The rubber from the tire draws heat to the plants. Ken said he has always relied on raised beds to rise above the cold, wet ground in his location.

Peat Pots and Plastic

Peat pots are another way to get a little extra out of the season. Tender plants, such as watermelon and cantaloupe, can be started indoors in these biodegradable pots. The pots can then be set in the garden when the weather gets nice. This way you don't lose any days when transplanting. You can combine peat pots with hot caps and black plastic to really extend the season on plants such as these that simply don't ripen (most seasons) if left to their own devices.

How to Enjoy Flowers Longer

The first year my wife got serious about growing annual and perennial flowers she was a little disappointed. She said it seemed by the time everything was planted and in bloom the season was coming to an end. That particular summer was a particularly short, cool summer. However she did have a point.

We can extend our season with flowers in a variety of ways. We can start our marigolds, zinnias and other annuals inside in early April while waiting patiently for our daffodils and tulips to bloom.

We can then plant hardy annuals such as petunias and snapdragons which can take a light frost. Meanwhile, the perennials will come up on their own. In the fall, our season is extended with fall flowering asters, sunflowers and hardy zin-

nias (which are actually perennials). We can also spend a lot of time in our gardens, after the flowers quit blooming, cutting back plants, thinning out flowers etc. Many perennials, annuals and herbs can then be brought inside if we so desire, so we can continue to enjoy our garden inside after the snow flies.

Like most northern gardeners, I get the most out of the short seasons by looking over the catalogs in January and February. Then I start a few plants indoors in March. In April and May I start to get my hands in the garden. I start out with the cool weather crops, garden throughout the summer, and pick well into October. During the winter months I can read and write about gardening. In **my** mind, I'm gardening year-round!

REFERENCES

—*Cold Climate Gardening*, Lewis Hill. Garden Way Publishing, 1987.

—*Garden's Alive!* Catalog of organic gardening products.

COPING WITH CRITTERS

As a garden columnist for *Above the Bridge Magazine* of Marquette, Michigan, I receive letters asking what to do about garden pests. One common concern is slugs. I haven't experienced a lot of problems with slugs in my garden for the following reasons (I think): either the chickens eat the slugs or I don't pay any attention to them. I can't help thinking it's more the work of the chickens and Mother Nature rather than not noticing the slugs. If they were in my garden I'm sure they would be having a feast—and demanding my attention (more on slugs later).

Garden pests, whether they be insects or animals, pose a problem for gardeners everywhere. However, after talking to folks from the north and the south I've come to the following conclusion: insects (except mosquitos, of course) aren't as bad in the northern states as they are in the southern states. The reason is the climate. According to northern New Hampshire Cooperative Extension entomologist Dr. Allan Eaton, climates with extended periods of cold weather like ours don't provide suitable habitat for a wide variety of insects.

Insecticides: Killing the Bugs Dead!

Fortunately, these days we're getting away from the DDTs and other chemicals that are potentially harmful to humans and animals. While saving the environment appears to be the "in thing" right now, it also makes good sense. There are simply too many people and animals to share too little earth with. So we've got to keep it free of contaminants. Besides, from my experience, I don't think we need to rely solely on chemical agents in our backyard gardens.

So much for my sermon on the environment. Let's get down to the business of protecting the crops we've toiled over all summer.

• • •

There are several products out on the market that make insect control safe and easy—but not necessarily cheap. That's why we need to combine organic insecticides and pesticides with strategic planting and other natural means to cope with our natural enemies.

One of the most popular and effective insecticides is rotenone. Rotenone is made from the refined roots of Asian and South American tropical plants. The 5% concentrate, which can be applied as a powder or liquid, will ward off aphids (which are partial to cabbage) cucumber beetles, flea beetles and even some bugs that go after fruit and berries, such as the apple maggot and blueberry maggot. Rotenone can be purchased from most hardware stores and nurseries in addition to the numerous seed catalogs available. Rotenone is recommended as an all purpose insecticide which will kill most garden insects.

Dipel is a "state of the art" moth and butterfly control formula. This insecticide, which is harmless to humans and animals, can be used right up until harvest time. Use Dipel if you're having particular problems with cabbage worms and loopers, (those little green worms found on cabbage, broccoli and other cole crops). The cabbage worm and looper is actually the larvae of a little white butterfly. So when you see these little critters fluttering around your garden, you know it's time to get out the Dipel.

Dipel is also used by market farmers and fruit growers. They use it to protect their crops from fruit tree worm pests. This product can also be used to kill the gypsy moths which infest forests as well as ornamental and fruit trees.

Safer's Insecticidal Soap is safe for both inside and outdoor use. This soap-like liquid is made up of fatty acid salts and contains no petroleum additives. With frequent use it will control aphids, whiteflies and spider mites on fruit trees, vegetables and ornamentals while leaving beneficial insects alone (do you ever wonder how it does this?).

Other Ways to Deal with Bugs

Other ways to control insects are by regular cultivation, crop rotation and companion planting. You can also help ward off the bugs by planting certain

plants, such as marigolds and garlic, among or near your cherished vegetables; the plants give out a pungent odor that discourages insects.

One way I compensate for insect damage is by planting several seeds, of say pumpkin, realizing I may loose a few plants (which I would have to thin out anyway) to insects.

Certainly the least toxic way of controlling insects is to pick them off the plants. Many gardeners go out at night and collect potato beetle bugs in a coffee can. You can also pick bugs off produce prior to cooking, unless of course, this doesn't agree with your taste buds. For instance, a good way to remove cabbage worms from broccoli is to soak the heads in cold water for a few hours. The cabbage worms will float to the top.

Now, back to the slugs. Organic Gardening (May/June 1992) solicited slug control tips from gardeners across the country including Oregon where natives claim the slug is the unofficial state animal. They came up with some amusing but apparently effective ways to deal with this critter. Here are a few of the more practical suggestions:

- Use a commercial sprayer with a long reach and spray your crops with a 50-50 mix of vinegar and water.

- A "trap crop" of mustard planted along the edge of your garden supposedly draws slugs away from your prized vegetables.

- Hand pick the slugs at night using a flashlight and feed them to your aquarium fish. According to the article, Linda and Bob Fleming of Springfield, Oregon gathered 7,148 slugs in just over two months this way. They kept daily tallies of their bounty.

- Pour a sand barrier around the base of your flowers.

- Go out after dark and torch 'em with a hand-held propane torch.

- And finally, to back up my claim about chickens, Sarah Dilworth of East Boothbay, Maine lets her chickens wonder in the garden before planting time. The chickens feast on the slugs and slug eggs.

Natural bug killers in this country are the swallows and bluebirds. These birds eat thousands of bugs each day. No garden should be without an easy-to-build swallow or bluebird house. Another tactic we can use to control insects is crop rotation. Potatoes in particular should not be planted year after year in the same spot. In fact, most crops should be rotated at least every other year.

Animal Pests

Unfortunately, what we gain by having fewer bugs, we lose to animal pests. Many folks in the North live in close proximity to the woods, making it easy for deer, bear, skunks, mice, porcupines, crows, woodchucks, raccoons, and an occasional moose to sneak in for a midnight snack.

Deer are generally wary of crossing open areas to feed in a backyard garden. However, crossing from the woods into a garden is a mere cakewalk for a whitetail. Deer visit gardens to browse through the corn mostly, but they've been known to stop and munch on just about anything. Luckily, deer usually don't get into my

Fencing in a garden is costly but necessary if your garden borders the woods.

garden until fall, after the bulk of my produce has been harvested. They sneak in at night, presumably, while my dog sleeps.

About the only thing you can do about deer, if they are a persistent problem, is to fence in your garden. This can be expensive. A cheaper alternative for folks who live in the country is to acquire a good watchdog.

Raccoons cause a lot of damage to corn. This animal is protected in some states, but can be live trapped with cages and sardines for bait. The Department of Natural Resources will often provide folks with live traps; they can also be purchased in seed catalogs. Here again I've been fortunate that raccoons wait until I've harvested most of my corn before they invade my garden.

Bears like corn too. If you've got a bear coming into your garden you've got a more serious problem than losing your produce. Chances are the bear is getting a little too brave which can become a dangerous situation. Consult your local natural resources agency to deal with this rather imposing creature.

Groundhogs are perhaps one of the most persistent—and destructive—garden pests to deal with. An adult groundhog can munch away a row of carrots in minutes. If one should saunter into your garden, or worse yet, set up an underground apartment in close proximity to your garden, you must act quickly to discourage this critter. The last time I had a groundhog move in near my garden I barricaded his hole immediately, which apparently discouraged him from taking up residency, as I never saw him again.

Other garden pests we must contend with in this country are horseflies and mosquitos. Although they leave our plants alone, they can drive the gardener right out of the garden!

REFERENCES

"15 Slug Stopping Strategies," compiled by Jill Jesiolowski, Organic Gardening, May/June 1992.

The Encyclopedia of Natural Insect & Disease Control, edited by Roger B. Yepsen, Jr., Rodale Press, Emmaus, Pennsylvania.

EEDS, WEEDS, WEEDS!

"Now tis the spring, and weeds are shallow-rooted.
Suffer them now and they'll o'ergrow the garden."

Shakespeare, King Henry VI

After ten years of gardening in the same location I could look back and recall the many fine gardens I'd grown; practically taste the fresh picked sweet corn and see the huge potato plants swaying in the breeze. But towards the end of that decade of gardening in the same spot I started to envision weeds. Weeds, weeds, weeds! The vision was real—weeds were choking my beloved garden!

Weeds love cool, wet summers. Quackgrass just loves it when you can't get the tiller through until late May; it has a chance to establish those stubborn rhizomes beneath the soil that are virtually impossible to conquer without an all-out assault with a rototiller or by physically removing them roots and all.

One summer I did just that. I devoted an entire summer to fighting weeds. At the end of the summer I was victorious over the weeds, although saddened that I had few fresh vegetables to eat. Besides tilling the garden once a week to kill off the inconspicuous, but stubborn root systems which had taken charge of my garden, I was able to clean up my asparagus patch, plant rhubarb, lime the garden (which was overdue), prune some trees and learn more about flower gardening.

The best strategy for weed control is to not let them get out of hand, which is easier said than done in these parts. With the help of fellow gardeners and good garden books, I've developed several strategies over the years to keep weeds at a minimum, or something I can live with.

North Country Gardening

by Neil Moran

Mulches

Mulches provide excellent weed control while trapping moisture and stabilizing the temperatures around your plants. Some types of mulches even provide food for plants. Mulches help reduce weeds by preventing their young seedlings from getting exposure to the air and sun.

However, be careful not to apply mulches too early in the spring. An early application of a thick mulch traps the cold air in the soil and consequently prohibits the release of heat to ward off a light frost. I usually don't apply a mulch until my plants are up and well established (sometimes as late as the first week in July).

Grass clippings are one of the most readily available mulches for town and country dwellers. A thick layer of grass clippings around your squash and certain flowers will provide a much needed respite from hoeing. However, it's a little impractical (but not impossible) to mulch long rows of vegetables with grass clippings.

Straw makes a good mulch and can be used to do a fairly long row. A tightly wrapped 75 lb. bale of straw will do a hundred foot row of corn, depending on how thick it is applied. Hay should be avoided unless it is mixed with manure and is well rotted. Unfortunately, mature hay contains the seeds for the weeds you're trying to get rid of!

Hay or straw mixed with manure is heavier and perhaps not practical to apply to a large area or long rows as a weed barrier. However, barn manure is indispensable as an organic fertilizer and humus builder. I use a manure mulch around my squash and pumpkins with the idea that nutrients will leach down into the root systems of these plants while smothering the weeds.

Some folks use mulch out of a compost bin. Again, this is a little heavier and messy to work with, thus perhaps not practical as a weed stopper for a large area. It's better to use compost as a soil conditioner. Apply it in the spring or fall and work it into the soil with a roto-tiller.

Newspaper and nonglossy magazines will provide a good barrier against those pesky weeds. Paper is light and easy to work with and usually available to the home

gardener. However, this can get messy. Newspapers and magazines can't be tilled under like grass clippings and the like. Nor can you readily remove newspapers and magazines from the garden at the end of the season as you would black plastic.

A good way to ward off the weeds while improving the soil is by planting cover crops. Cover crops such as rye, hairy vetch and buckwheat will choke out the weeds and improve the soil when they are turned under (see section titled "Cover Crops for the North).

Cultivation and Hoeing

I find it relaxing doing a little hoeing as the evening sun wanes on a warm day in the North Country. On these quiet evenings I've even heard loons yodelling on the river. However, hoeing is no fun if you've got row upon excruciatingly long row of stubborn weeds to chunk away at until your hands blister.

Here's where a little machinery comes in handy. Whether you've got a front-end tiller, a rear-tine tiller, or even a hand cultivator like grandpa once used, it's a lot easier to cultivate between your rows of peas, beans and cucumbers than it is to hoe. Keep this in mind when you plant to be sure you space your rows wide enough to accommodate the appropriate machinery. Of course, folks with small gardens don't have to worry about this—all they really need is a hoe.

I usually don't mulch my long rows of corn, beans and peas; this requires more organic material than I'm willing to wheel out to the garden. So I space my rows far enough apart to get my 24" wide tiller down through the rows. Needless to say, this saves me a wheelbarrow load of work. Even then I need to do this once every couple of weeks during the summer to stay ahead of the quackgrass, lamb's quarter and glasswort.

I use my grandfather's old push cultivator to get between my short rows of carrots, beets and lettuce. This method of cultivation works well (and is good exercise) if done regularly.

It's important to work up your garden a few times in the spring and fall. In the low lying area where I live near the river it is virtually impossible to work the garden more than a couple of times (if I'm lucky) in the fall due to the heavy rains.

Plastic and Chemical Weed Controls

Black plastic is a practical though somewhat expensive way to hold back the weeds. A 10 X 25 ft. roll of black plastic costs around $5.00. The advantage of plastic is your plants also get a boost from the warmth the plastic attracts. One disadvantage of black plastic is it requires a little fussing. It can be somewhat of a hassle cutting out holes to plant the seeds or transplants. And in the fall it can be a real bear trying to find your black sheeting under all the plant growth. However, when used as a weed deterrent and season extender it can't be beat!

The herbicide Round-up can save a lot of hoeing and pulling weeds for the busy gardener. This liquid weed-killer must be applied on a warm (70 degrees or warmer) day. You'll have to wait at least a week to see the results. The advantage of a chemical spray is you can get in close to perennial plants like asparagus or between decorative stones and kill off otherwise hard to get at weeds. Always use protective gloves and a face mask when working with this and other chemical weed killers.

The above methods of eliminating weeds work best if used in conjunction with each other. The important thing is not to let weeds go to seed. I assure you, they will give way to a multitude of offspring! Also, try to stay ahead of this rather challenging game by weeding on a regular basis rather than procrastinating (like I have) and be faced with the overwhelming task of hoeing a weed choked garden!

A little hoeing is good therapy. However, you don't want to get too much of a good thing. Doctor's orders.

REFERENCES

—*Down to Earth Vegetable Gardening Know-How*, Dick Raymond, Garden Way Publishing, 1975.

COVER CROPS FOR THE NORTH

The first few gardens I planted after we bought our home in the country were magnificent. It was partially due to some great weather we experienced those years. However, I believe it could also be attributed to the fact I was planting in previously fallow soil where cows once roamed. About a decade later my luck, and my plants, started to noticeably suffer (the weather didn't help much either).

That's when I discovered "green manure."

Granular fertilizers will get your plants off and running but they don't add anything to your soil texture. After several years of relying solely on inorganic or chemical fertilizer, the soil will turn hard and loose its "tilth." A garden has good tilth if you can squeeze a ball of dirt in your hand and it will compact like a snowball.

Green manure—or cover crops—improve soil by adding organic matter and nitrogen to the soil. Planting cover crops should be part of your soil improvement plans. As you harvest, or take from the earth, so must you return nutrients back to the soil. Growing cover crops is also a form of crop rotation. For instance, each year you can relieve a section in the garden by planting one of the cover crops suggested below. This way, you still have vegetables to eat each year while eventually improving the entire garden.

If your garden is severely depleted of nutrients and organic matter or is engulfed by weeds (or is generally looking forlorn!) give the entire garden a rest for a season and plant nothing but cover crops. Or you can wait until late summer and sow a cover crop, such as vetch, oats or rye grass (or all three) after you've harvested everything else. Simply till it all under when you work the soil in the spring.

COVER CROPS

Common Name	Soil Preference	Lime Requirements	Seeding Rate (lbs./1000 sq. ft.)	Depth to Cover Seed	When to Sow	When to Turn Under
Buckwheat	Widely Adaptable	Low	1-1/2	3/4	Late Spring and Summer	Summer or Fall
Clover: Alsike	Heavy Loams	Med	1/4	1/2	Spring	Fall
Oats	Widely Adaptable	Low	2-1/2	1	Spring	Summer or Fall
Rye, Spring	Widely Adaptable	Low	2	3/4	Spring	Summer
Rye, Winter	Widely Adaptable	Low	2	3/4	Fall	Spring
Sweet Clover Common White	Heavy Loams	High	1/2	1/2	Spring	Fall
Vetch Hairy	Widely Adaptable	Low	1-1/2	3/4	Spring	Fall

There are other reasons for planting cover crops. Cover crops provide food for earthworms, add humus to the soil and will reach deep down into the earth and absorb nutrients from the ground which can then be worked into the top layer of the soil. Cover crops are also an environmentally sound replacement for inorganic fertilizers. The USDA reports that a good winter growth of a legume such as hairy vetch will easily replace the nitrogen needed to raise a crop of corn.

BUCKWHEAT Here is a good choice for a cover crop. Buckwheat grows a leafy foliage that will add an abundance of organic material to the soil when it is tilled under. The flowers are also quite pretty. Buckwheat is particularly beneficial for older gardens that are severely depleted of organic matter. It will grow in virtually

any soil type or condition: clay, sand, wet and dry. But be careful you don't let it go to seed or you'll have buckwheat growing everywhere! Buckwheat is sown in the spring and tilled under in late summer or fall.

RYE GRASS Annual rye grass can be planted anytime. Rye will choke out other plants so it's a good choice if weeds are a problem. Annual rye grass can be planted either in late spring and be tilled under in the fall, or planted in late summer and be tilled under the following spring.

LEGUMES Alfalfa, alsike clover, lupine and hairy vetch are all legumes which actually extract nitrogen from the air and convert it into a form usable by plants. Farmers have long recognized the value of alfalfa as a soil builder. Most feed stores carry alfalfa.

Planting a Cover Crop

You don't need expensive machinery to plant a cover crop. Simply work up the section where you intend to plant then broadcast the seed by hand over that area. Cover the seed the best you can with a garden rake. Be careful not to sow the seed too thickly which can cause stunted growth of the cover crop. Cover large seeds such as oats, wheat and buckwheat with about an inch of soil; the smaller seeds, such as clover should be covered with one half inch of soil.

REFERENCES

Down-to-Earth Vegetable Garden Know-How, by Dick Raymond, Garden Way Publishing, 1975.

ULTURE FOR INDIVIDUAL VEGETABLES

SPARAGUS

One price check at the supermarket should convince you to give asparagus a try in your garden. If you've got the room to grow it by all means do so. It grows quite well in cold climates. Twenty crowns, or roots of asparagus will provide a few meals for a family of four. If you don't have room right in the garden for asparagus, set aside a space in your lawn to grow this delectable vegetable.

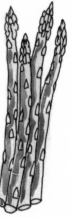

Asparagus is a perennial that grows well in a sandy loam type soil. First, locate a sunny spot in your garden or yard that provides good soil drainage. Asparagus won't tolerate a soggy location.

Next, prepare the bed by working some well rotted manure into the soil. This will be your only chance to really mulch underneath your plants. Asparagus will occupy a location for over 20 years.

Now you're ready to plant. Most folks prefer to plant the asparagus crowns. Planting crowns will yield table ready asparagus much sooner than starting by seed.

Male plants tend to produce more spears than female plants; female plants waste energy producing seed. Hybrid male plants were developed to increase asparagus yields. Jersey Knight is an example of a mostly male variety. It is not only a prolific producer of tasty green spears but it resists fusarium and rust diseases. Mary Washington is an old standby that holds its flavor after the spears appear. It is sold in most garden catalogs.

Asparagus is planted in the spring. Find a mostly sunny location with a soil pH around 7.0. Dig a trench 6-8 inches below ground level. Lay the roots out flat and cover with 1-2 inches of good top soil. Space the plants about 16 inches apart

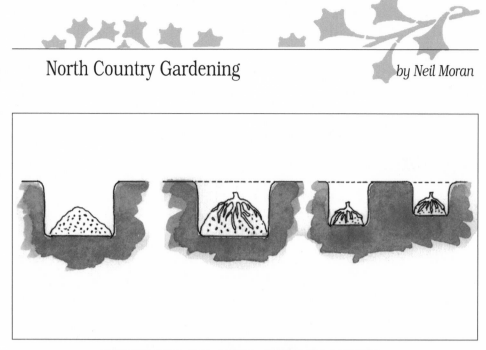

HOW TO PLANT ASPARAGUS:

1. *Make a mound of soil, well rotted livestock manure and an inorganic fertilizer and fill hole halfway to the top.*
2. *Spread the asparagus roots over the mound. Fill about half way to the top with soil. Continue to fill the hole gradually as the plant starts to appear above the ground.*
3. *Asparagus can also be planted at different depths to vary the harvest time.*

in the trench. Gradually fill in the hole as the spears begin to grow out of the trench (this will occur over a period of weeks). Eventually, you will have filled the hole to ground level. You may even want to heap the soil over the top of the trench and around the plant to allow water to run off.

The first year after your initial planting will be spent watching for the spears to poke through the surface of the ground. Let these grow. Now is a good time to mulch around the spears with leaves, grass clippings or straw. I lay the mulch on thick to prevent the weeds from sprouting, which can ruin a nice patch of asparagus if allowed to get out of hand. The spears will continue to grow into a tall bushy plant. Wait until the following spring to remove the dead plants from the garden.

This is also a good time to apply a little fertilizer of your choice. About 10 pounds of a 12-12-12 fertilizer for every 250 square feet of plants is sufficient for the year. Or, apply a generous application of "manure tea" several times during the early part of the summer.

By the second year (two years after your initial planting) you can start watching for the purplish heads to appear. The young spears, which usually start to appear in mid-May in this country, are a real harbinger of spring. Cut the shoots off at the base of the spears with a sharp pocket knife. It may take a few cuttings to get a feel for when to harvest this vegetable; avoid harvesting shoots that have turned tough (which can happen quickly in warm weather).

It's important, especially with a small patch of asparagus, to check for new spears daily. They shoot out of the ground rapidly when the weather gets warm. You'll need all the spears you can

Alan Alexander prepares an asparagus bed in Erin Ontario. He filled the bed with a humus rich compost.

get to feed three or four people. It's surprising how much I actually get out of my two ten foot rows of asparagus.

Asparagus will keep in the refrigerator for a few days while you cut a few more to make up a meal. The kids might even like this vegie. I like to eat the shoots raw (of course, I've been known to eat a potato raw too!). The young shoots have a perceptible sweet taste.

Each time I look at the price of asparagus in the store I'm tempted to grow enough to market myself. Or just give it away to friends. I bet I'd have a lot of friends!

EANS: *Green and Wax*

Fresh creamed beans are a real summer delight—and one we can appreciate early. Beans are easy to grow, prolific producers and a good source of vitamins. My wife used to complain that I grew too many beans. She was right. But I just couldn't help myself. I marvelled at the amount of produce you get for so little effort, in comparison to other vegetables.

These days I save garden space and picking time by growing only what I'll need for a few meals and canning and freezing—and what I give to friends and family.

The biggest problem with beans in the cold climates is those extended days of rainy, cool weather which can occur just about any time during the summer. It's particularly a problem if it occurs when the bean pods are starting to form on the plant. Cool, wet weather will cause the developing pods, especially yellow beans, to form a rust or even rot on the vine.

You should never disturb the leaves of the plant during wet conditions due to the possibility of spreading disease. However, during extended days of soggy weather (the type that forms a green fungus on the top of your soil) it is necessary to take some kind of action to save your beans. You can minimize this type of damage by shaking the water off of the plants with a broom. This will also expose the underside of the plant to the wind and sun.

Beans generally don't require a lot of dusting for insects. The major insects that prey on beans are the leaf hopper and bean leaf beetle. These can be effectively controlled with liquid rotenone. Nor do beans require fertilizer and they actually return nitrogen to the soil. After you've harvested your beans till them into the soil or throw them on a compost pile; spread them on the garden later.

Plant beans when all danger of frost is past. They're not a hardy plant and even a light frost will kill the young plants. Here in Northern Michigan, where we can expect a frost as late as June 15, I wait until around the 10th of June to sow beans. This still allows lots of time for a mid-August harvest. You can also space the harvest by successive planting (it also gives your back a time to rest between pickings) every couple of weeks.

Plant beans two-three inches apart in rows at least 18 inches wide. This should allow enough room to cultivate between the rows. My father always said you should lay the seed in the ground with the little hash mark facing the sky, rather than just plunking the seed in the ground. I've tried both methods without noticing any significant difference in germination.

One way to improve your bean harvest is to use an organic inoculant. This will neutralize the nitrogen in the soil by placing billions of live rhizobia bacteria into your soil. Dust it right into your furrows as you plant your seed. An inoculant can be purchased in a rather large quantity (9 oz.) which will be enough to do a 150 ft. row. Smaller amounts can be purchased for the backyard or patio garden.

There are as many varieties of beans to choose from as there are jack pines in the North Country. I've stuck pretty close to Tendercrop in the green bean variety and Kentucky Wonder Wax (especially good in northern climates) in the yellow variety. Provider and Venture are a good bet if you have trouble growing green beans in your northern location. Other yellow beans worth experimenting with include Goldkist and Earliwax Golden Yellow.

Some beans freeze better and are more rust resistant than others. However, they're all pretty easy to grow so you shouldn't have to go without buttered green or yellow beans either way.

RY BEANS

A diet of dry beans will provide an excellent source of protein without all the cholesterol found in red meat. However, dry beans may not be practical for the gardener with limited space (and time).

These beans grow pretty much like the other bean types; that is, they have to be planted after the danger of frost is past and are affected by the same diseases and bug types.

The major difference is at harvest time. Leave the plants in the ground until most of the leaves have dried and fallen away, then pull them up by the roots. Hang the beans in a dry place to finish the drying process. This will usually take place in September.

When drying is complete and the seeds are ready to fall out of the pods, the threshing begins. Dry beans can be shelled by hand, like peas—or, flail the whole plant back and forth in a barrel until all of the beans have fallen out of the pods.

Growing dry beans is like collecting stamps. There are at least a dozen open-pollinated and heirloom varieties in assorted colors to choose from. Northern gardeners can have fun growing (and collecting) the many different dry beans on the market. You may want to trade your different bean types with your neighbors!

Jacob's Cattle or Trout is a pretty red-specked heirloom that matures early. It is kidney shaped and excellent for making soups and baking. Soldier is a Maine heirloom. It gets its name from the red-brown figure of a soldier on its eye. This one is good in stews and for baked beans. Also worth mentioning is the Great

Northern white bean. This is an heirloom bean grown by the Mandan Indians. It arrived on the garden and agricultural scene after 1907.

Dry beans are perhaps something better left to the "advanced gardener" or at least one with some time on their hands, such as a retiree. Between selecting the many interesting varieties, planting and harvesting, a person won't have much time for the ol' rocking chair!

OLE BEANS

Italians and other European immigrants to the North Country are noted for growing the pole bean variety. Pole beans grow skyward on a trellis, instead of in long rows. Thus, they're a good space saver for small gardens. Pole beans are fairly easy to grow and like other bean types, prolific producers.

Pole beans need some type of wire or nylon mesh trellis to cling to as they make their reach for the sky. A nylon or fabric trellis won't burn the vines (like wire mesh or fencing) and is fairly easy to work with. These are fairly inexpensive and can be purchased from nursery catalogs. And of course, you can construct your own trellis out of wood and string or fabric mesh.

HOW TO STAKE POLE BEANS: *Here's an easy way to stake pole beans. Binder twine or string can be strung vertically and horizontally. Pole beans can climb these easily.*

Plant pole beans directly into the ground when all danger of frost is past. Dig a one inch trench and space the seeds about three inches apart along the base of the trellis. Soil temperature for all beans should be at least 60 degrees at the time of planting.

A good choice for pole beans is the hardy Northeaster, Vermont Cranberry Pole Bean (60 days to maturity) and the classic favorite, Romano Italian pole bean.

One advantage pole beans have over the low lying bush varieties is they don't suffer from prolonged periods of wet weather. However, wind can be a problem if you're planting in open areas, thus, make sure the trellis you purchase or construct is up to the task.

LIMA BEANS

You'll need all the tricks you can muster to grow this one in the frigid zones, unless you're living in a warmer "microclimate."

Start with careful seed selection. Fordhook (a large seeded variety) and Geneva (a baby lima bean) are two lima bean varieties favored by northerners. The latter is suggested for folks who have had difficulty growing this protein rich staple. Both require about 85 days to mature, which really is pushing it in the northern tier states that border Canada.

The difference between Fordhook and Geneva is that the latter is more likely to germinate in cooler temperatures. While most lima varieties require warm soil for germination, Geneva will germinate in soil 10 degrees cooler than lima beans usually require, thus extending the season by a couple of weeks.

Like peppers and tomatoes, lima beans need warmth—and a fairly long growing season. Here's where row covers may be worth the investment if you really want lima beans. The reusable row covers will trap in warmth and protect the developing pods from strong, cool breezes.

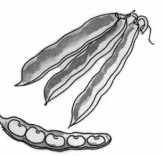

Lima beans are sown much like green and wax beans. An organic inoculant is recommended (see Beans: Green and Wax) to push this one along. I also resort to using a little "booster," mixing a 12-12-12 complete fertilizer into the soil prior to planting. I then side dress a couple of times over the course of the summer. A half pound of 12-12-12 is sufficient to side dress a thirty foot row of limas. If you like lima beans, or simply like a challenge, give this one a try. Then let me know how you're doing!

EETS

Red beets are "North Country friendly." That is, when all else fails to produce, you should still get a healthy crop of beets to harvest. In fact, beets tend to flourish in the cool, wet climate common in our region.

The first year I had a garden of my own I ordered the Detroit Perfected red beets; I've had nary a reason to try another variety. I don't know where they got their name, but this beet won't leave you hanging whether you're in Detroit, Michigan or Portland, Maine. However, if you're looking for a little flair in your beets, try Chioggia. You'll find the pink and white flesh pleasing to the eye and your palate.

Don't take beets for granted, like I once did. Over the years I have come to appreciate the fine qualities beets possess. They're easy to grow, provide nutritious

greens and store quite well, particularly the Perfected Detroit I mentioned. Beets are also quite bug resistant.

Sow beets by hand by gently patting a thin layer of soil over the tiny seeds. When the plants start to appear, gradually thin them over a four week period by plucking the smaller plants, initially, then thin back to three or four inches apart; the further they're thinned apart, the larger they'll grow.

Leave beets in the ground right up until the snow flies— they will keep much longer in your cellar or crawl space if you do so. The only drawback you should be aware of is beets tend to be a little muddy when you harvest them late in the fall. Dry them by spreading them out on the floor of your garage or tool shed. Stir them around every other day with a broom until they're completely dry.

The best way to store beets, or any root crop, is to spread them out as much as possible. If I've got the room, I like to spread them right out on the floor. Otherwise, I store them in wooden boxes and bushel baskets which requires periodic turning to ensure the beets don't spoil.

Beets are delicious boiled and served with butter or pickled and served with just about any meat entree. Once you get hooked on them you'll look forward to them year after year.

BROCCOLI

Broccoli provided comic relief from politics during George Bush's presidency. Mr. Bush's reluctance to eat broccoli caused a national stir. As well it should. Broccoli is one of the most nutritious vegetables we can eat.

More important news for you and me (yes, more important than a president's fussy eating habits) is broccoli's known cancer fighting ability. Researchers at

Johns Hopkins University School of Medicine revealed that broccoli, and other crucifer crops, are high in sulforaphane, an inducer of enzymes that detoxify carcinogens in the body.

The **best** news about broccoli is that it's right at home here in the North. It is easy to grow, requires only a handful of good growing days, and can withstand a heavy frost. I've picked broccoli spears well into October with a layer of snow under my feet!

Alan Alexander of Erin, Ontario can't wait for the taste of broccoli. He starts his Goliath broccoli in a large greenhouse. Even though he has had snow in April, the broccoli inside the greenhouse is thriving in the 90 degree temperature. Towards the end of April he sets his broccoli (and other plants) outside under glass cloches. One year he said he was eating broccoli by the 18th of June!

Goliath broccoli (photo courtesy of Alan Alexander)

North Country Gardening

by Neil Moran

Broccoli can be sown directly into the garden or started as transplants. I sprinkle broccoli seeds along a 15 foot row, planting only about a half inch deep. I then sprinkle soil over the seeds and pat the furrow down with my hand.

I've had great luck growing Hybrid Green Comet and Packman. Another variety, said to be particularly high in cancer fighting sulforaphane, is Saga. While this broccoli type grows huge heads, it will go to seed faster than other varieties.

When the seedlings are about two inches high, I thin them back a little, but not too much. I've had a great deal of luck digging up the developing plants (when they've reached 4-5 inches high) and transplanting them to a different location in the garden.

A little manure tea applied during the course of the summer will provide enough nutrients to see these plants through. Keep an eye out for insects, particularly cabbage worms, which may be working on the leaves of the plants. An application or two of rotenone should address this problem. Also, when you harvest broccoli you should soak the spears in cold water for a couple hours (any remaining cabbage worms will rise to the top).

It's important to harvest broccoli when it first heads up. If you wait too long the heads turn seedy and taste bitter. Simply cut off the heads with a sharp knife. The plant will continue to produce smaller bunches of broccoli. This vegetable is one of the most prolific producers. It just keeps going right up until the snow literally buries it!

Broccoli requires very little blanching time and freezes quite well. Kids (and some presidents) aren't particularly fond of broccoli. My kids got interested in eating it by calling it "trees." I guess they thought it was neat eating a tree.

Perhaps if the former president had eaten his broccoli . . .

RUSSELS SPROUTS

I used to think Brussels sprouts were kind of weird—not just to eat—but to look at. I was in my teens at the time and probably thought a lot of things were weird. Today, I think Brussels sprouts are far from weird; they're nutritious and they taste darn good.

Brussels sprouts are hardy. They've earned the gardener's respect by performing well year after year. They're easy to start from seed in flats or by planting directly into the garden. Oliver and Prince Marvel will yield early Brussels sprouts. For a later harvest, plant the hybrid Jade E Cross. Brussels sprouts will take a light frost in spring and you can dust the snow from them in late fall for a tasty meal of buttered sprouts.

Start the seeds indoors in late April to early May in peat pots or cell type containers. Brussels sprout seeds are tiny and fragile, that's why I prefer to start them indoors. Be careful not to let the plants get away from you in the pots. I usually hold off until May to start mine inside. By the first of June you'll have Brussels sprouts to set out.

If you choose to plant them directly into the garden, choose a site where the soil is especially soft and fine. It's also best to plant when the weather is fairly mild.

After your sprouts sprout and are about five or six inches tall you may wish to transplant them down the row to space them out. Eventually space to about eighteen inches between each plant. Transplanting may slow the plant down slightly, but it won't matter since Brussels sprouts can grow well into the fall, thus they have lots of time to mature.

As the plants become bushy and leafy, I cut back the long stems that support the leaves. This discourages slugs from clinging to the wet undersides. Sometimes I use these leaves to cover my newly formed cauliflower to prevent them from becoming bleached by the sun. Otherwise, they go into a compost pile. You can also lay them down between your rows of vegetables to act as a mulch to keep weeds from poking through.

The best time to harvest Brussels sprouts is in the fall. I usually wait until after the first frost—often later. Get a comfortable spot to sit and pluck these little cabbages off the stems. It's tedious work but can be enjoyable sitting outside on a sunny fall day on the edge of your garden plucking sprouts. And don't mind the slugs, they don't bite. Simply pick them off the plant (they don't freeze worth a darn!) as you continue this chore. The huge plants make excellent compost but will need to sit over the winter to decompose.

Brussels sprouts freeze pretty well and are excellent in a cheese sauce with a little salt and pepper sprinkled over them.

By the way, my kids don't like Brussels sprouts. They say they're weird.

ABBAGE

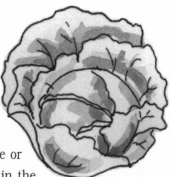

Some like it hot, some like it not. Cabbage falls in the latter category. That's why cabbage, like most cole crops, such as cauliflower and broccoli, grows quite well in the cold climate zones.

Cabbage is easy to start from seed in the house or greenhouse, four or five weeks prior to setting out in the garden. In fact, some care must be taken to avoid letting the transplants get too

Wisconsin All-Season Cabbage

large and spindly before it's time to set them outside. This can be avoided by waiting until at least late April to start the seed and by using a grow light (see "Starting from Seed).

Cabbage will make the transition from window or greenhouse to the garden quite well. Very little hardening off needs to take place with cabbage.

It is best to set cabbage out during the last week of May or first week of June, when it is still relatively cool. Transplant on an overcast day. The hot sun has frustrated many of my efforts to start cabbage. However, I've discovered one trick to cope with the hot sun. Cover the young plants with straw or paper (not plastic) for a day or two after transplanting until they get established and can withstand the heat of the sun.

Plant cabbage about 18 inches apart in rows about two feet apart. Cabbage attracts insects. And how! The cabbage worm, cabbage looper and aphids do the most damage. My problems are usually with the little green cabbage loopers. If left unchecked they'll leave your cabbage looking like it was riddled with buck shot. The cabbage looper first appears as a white butterfly fluttering around your garden. It's a harbinger of the danger that lies ahead! These critters can be eliminated with a toxic chemical dust such as Sevin. However, I prefer a nontoxic bioinsecticide with the trade name MVP. Dipel is another good nontoxic exterminator for the dreaded cabbage looper. You can also resort to row covers which are very effective at preventing insects from gaining access to your plants.

The important thing is don't wait until the bugs have drilled holes in your wannabe prize cabbage—start dusting or spraying immediately after your plants are well established in your garden.

Cabbage aren't big feeders. In fact, if forced to grow too rapidly the big beautiful heads tend to crack. I suggest you work some organic matter into the ground first; later, you can sidedress with a little fertilizer or manure tea.

I've had luck storing cabbage by wrapping the heads tightly in newspaper and placing in a cool, dry place. A few recipes, such as frozen coleslaw and sauerkraut, will also give you something to do with your surplus cabbage. Cabbage has a high vitamin content so it's well worth the effort to grow this vegetable in your garden.

CARROTS

Carrots remind me of kids; when a child comes into my garden they head straight for the carrots! That's one reason I grow lots of carrots. Kids can't resist pulling a bright orange carrot out of the ground.

Another reason to grow carrots is because when everything else goes wrong in this harsh climate—late frosts in June, early frosts in August, cool nights, too wet,—carrots come through. Some of the worst summers in this region produce the best carrots. Like most root crops, carrots thrive in cool, wet weather. Thus, most years I have a bumper crop!

There's a nice assortment of carrots out there to choose from. My favorite pastime during the winter months is to sit with a hot cup of coffee and browse through my garden catalogs. The colorful pages, accented by the orange carrots, will brighten up the most dismal winter day.

The Nantes variety is probably the most popular carrot due to its high yields and slender appearance. However, there's more to choose from such as Tendersweet (suitable for fair exhibits), the uniform Minicor and the gourmet Little Finger (midget) variety.

Carrots need the most attention prior to planting. The soil should be worked especially fine. Carrots can take up to two weeks or better to germinate, thus weeds often get a jump on the carrots and will choke them out. This can be avoided by choosing a spot in the garden that is free of rhizomes (underground root systems) and hasn't been recently fertilized with manure.

Sow the tiny seeds only about a 1/4 of an inch deep. Firmly pat some fine soil over top of the furrow with your hand. When the carrots are 2-3 inches high, begin thinning by gradually plucking a few carrots here and there for a few weeks as the carrots grow taller. You can avoid disturbing the fragile plant by plucking a few at a time.

Another way to plant carrots comes from Sault Ste. Marie, Ontario. Canadian gardener Ross Mervyn suggests mixing carrot seed with radish seeds. This will help prevent the tiny carrot plants from crowding each other. Also, the mature radishes help keep the soil loose around the carrots. And finally, radishes germinate much quicker than carrots, thus you can locate where your carrots have been planted. This is particularly helpful when the weeds start to sprout up around your carrots, which have yet to appear above the ground.

There's a new carrot seed type out on the market (offered by Johnny's Selected Seed) that promises to eliminate the tedious task of thinning. Of course, you pay for the convenience. Some clever gardener decided to coat the seed into a ball that is easy to handle. These tablets are an especially good choice for elderly or disabled folks and children who might have difficulty handling the tiny seed. The seed could also be spaced further apart, thus eliminating the need to bend over to thin the tiny plants.

If your garden is rich in organic matter you shouldn't need any fertilizer to help your carrots along. In fact, I've had carrots crack as a result of inorganic fertilizers. Apparently, the nitrogen in the fertilizer causes a growth spurt that is too rapid, causing the carrots to crack in a spiral fashion down the length of the carrot.

Carrots need regular thinning the first month or so after they appear above ground. I like to thin a little at a time, disturbing the fragile plants as little as possible. Keep the weeds plucked around your carrots. Also, get in fairly close with your hoe or garden fork after the carrots are 6-7 inches tall. You'll not only eliminate the weeds, but loosen the soil around the carrots and discourage root maggots and cutworms.

Carrots can remain in the ground late into the fall. I like to start picking the tiny carrots in early August—pick right up until the snow flies—then dig the remaining carrots and store them in my crawl space. Carrots will keep for several months if stored properly (see chapter on storing vegetables).

Carrots are fun to grow. I'm always amazed to see this bright orange vegetable come out of the cold black earth. Perhaps it brings out the child in me.

CAULIFLOWER

Mark Twain once described cauliflower as "cabbage with a college education." This sophisticated vegetable is fairly easy to grow; however, it's sensitive to extremes in temperatures. Extremes of heat or cold can cause this member of the cabbage family to set a stunted head. Therefore, I suggest you plant an early and late crop of cauliflower.

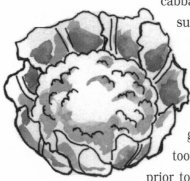

Cauliflower can be started indoors or directly seeded in the garden. I've tried both methods with equal success. Cauliflower will grow quickly in a greenhouse, so don't start them too early. I usually start mine four to six weeks prior to setting them outside. When the plants reach

about four or five inches tall, transplant to a sunny location in the garden. Do this in the evening to avoid direct exposure to the sun the first day which can cause your fledgling cauliflower to wilt and get off to a poor start. Cauliflower can be transplanted any time before or after the last probable frost.

Snow King Cauliflower

If sowing directly into the garden I prefer to plant when the weather has settled a bit, perhaps the last week in May or first week in June. When the plants reach 3-4 inches tall thin them to at least 18 inches apart. You can carefully dig the plants up at this time and move them down the row.

Cauliflower needs to be blanched by protecting the developing heads from the sun. Otherwise, the heads will turn yellow and tough. This is accomplished by simply taking the leaves of the plant and tying them together above the head. Or, the leaves can be plucked from the plant and tucked in around the head. Either method will produce a white, tender and delicious cauliflower for supper.

Cauliflower and other cole crops are more prone to bugs than other vegetables. Caution is in order, however—if you use chemical pesticides—don't apply too close to harvest time. Warning labels on chemical powders and sprays will indicate when to quit applying a product prior to eating the vegetable.

Over the years I've discovered it's unnecessary to resort strictly to chemical insecticides to treat cauliflower (or any vegetable for that matter). Rotenone powder will take care of the aphids and other insects which bother cauliflower. Dipel will take care of cabbage loopers which may visit your cauliflower plants. There are also a number of nontoxic means to deal with slugs (see section on critters).

It doesn't take a college education to grow cauliflower. However, you may feel a bit sophisticated yourself when you display a big white fluffy cauliflower for a county fair exhibit or show it off to your neighbor!

CELERY

My wife brought home some celery plants one time for me to try in the garden. I was pessimistic at first. Later, I was pleasantly surprised when the plants produced thick stalks of celery.

Celery gets overlooked in this land of snow. Yet, I've grown celery from transplants with the ease of snowshoeing across an open field. I grow celery in a sandy loam type soil which is ideal. Celery may be too difficult to grow in clay or sand. If you have these soil types, work in some organic matter right into the rows where you'll be planting your celery. Then expect to fertilize your plants at two or three

week intervals with a manure tea or 12-12-12 fertilizer. You should also apply a thick mulch around the base of your plants.

Celery must be started indoors (or purchase transplants from a nursery). Ventura is a popular celery variety which requires 80 days to maturity. Start seeds 10-12 weeks before setting them outside. Sprinkle celery seed into a fine starting mixture and cover with 1\8 of an inch of soil. You'll need a grow light to start celery plants. When the plant develops two true leaves, transplant to cell type containers. Move them to the garden in late May to mid-June when the weather is warm and settled. Choose a spot in the garden rich in organic matter as celery requires a rich growing medium.

Celery will tolerate hot days; however, it's best to water celery during a prolonged hot, dry spell. We generally don't experience extended periods of hot dry weather in the North, thus this region is favorable for growing this versatile vegetable.

Celery also requires blanching which is done by hilling the plant around the stalks so only the leaves appear above the ground. Blanching will give the celery a mild taste and a whitish appearance. However, you don't **have** to blanch celery. The green stalks of unblanched celery are a little stronger to the taste, perhaps all the better to flavor your favorite venison stew or vegetable soup.

Celery can be harvested in late summer or early fall and be stored much like carrots. This vegetable will keep as long as carrots do if stored properly. It requires a storage area with high humidity and near freezing temperatures to store well.

Many greenhouses and nurseries don't carry celery. If this is the case you may ask the proprietor to offer this overlooked yet suitable-to-the-North vegetable.

SWEET CORN

Waves lapping on the beach. A warm summer breeze. Baseball on the radio. The smell of barbecued chicken.

And sweet corn.

The taste of sweet corn is a taste of summer. You get a taste of summer each time you bite into a deliciously hot, buttery ear of sweet corn. No other vegetable can do this.

Many northerners don't grow sweet corn in their gardens, or have trouble doing so. Some

North Country Gardening

by Neil Moran

Hybrid Sunglow Sweet Corn

folks think the growing season is too short for sweet corn or that it simply takes up too much space in the garden.

To address the latter concern first, one 30 foot row of sweet corn will yield over 45 ears of corn. But if you still think your garden is too small you may want to try "compatibility planting" as practiced by the Chippewa, Potawatomi and other American Indians. These Indians conserve space and enrich Mother Earth by planting squash and beans in tight with their sweet corn. Just make sure the squash gets plenty of sunshine. By planting the "three sisters" in this fashion it not only conserves space but the beans, when worked under in the fall, add nitrogen to the soil.

The other concern I hear from folks has to do with the short growing season in the cold climate zones. Many different varieties, hybrids mostly, were developed to shorten the days to maturity needed to put sweet corn on the table. To ensure the sweet corn you've planted gets on your dinner table, choose a variety that requires less than 70 days to mature.

There are several seed and nursery companies which offer varieties of sweet corn suitable for the North. My favorite, and most consistent producer of ripe sweet corn, is Hybrid Sunglow. This variety has never left my tongue wagging at the end of the season. The petite ears are sweet and excellent for freezing.

Gurney's offers some varieties which take slightly longer to mature, are larger and sweeter, and have been grown successfully where I live. For example, Hybrid Sunburst Sweet Corn requires 70 days to maturity. Its eight inch ears are a little sweeter than the Sunglow variety. It should be sown rather early (mid to last week of May if the weather is favorable) to avoid falling victim to a mid-September frost. Folks in the Eastern Upper Peninsula of Michigan where I live have been growing Early Yellow Hybrid Bantam successfully for years. It also requires 70 good growing days and will produce a rather large, sweet ear of corn.

Work the ground well before planting. A slightly sandy soil won't hurt your chances with sweet corn. It's a good idea to work some well rotted nitrogen-rich manure, like sheep or chicken manure, into your potential corn patch prior to planting. Plant corn an inch or two apart in rows at least 18 inches apart. The earlier corn is planted in this region the better; corn will withstand a mild frost, but be careful. The last week of May is probably the best time to sow corn in the North. Expect to harvest the last week of August or early September. In the area where I live it's not unusual to get a frost in mid to late August. If my corn is fully developed and healthy it will withstand a little dip below freezing. A hard frost is a bit more of a challenge.

Keep the rows as weed free as possible by shallow cultivating or hoeing. You can also use a mulch, such as straw or grass clippings, to control the weeds between the rows. It's best to mulch no sooner than the middle of July when the soil is drier and warmer.

About this time you can also side dress your corn with a 12-12-12 granular fertilizer or spread well rotted chicken or sheep manure between the rows and work it in just below the surface. To apply a granular fertilizer, make a shallow furrow about 6-8 inches from either side of the corn. Sprinkle 12-12-12 fertilizer in the furrow, then cover with soil. Then step back and watch it take off!

Watch for corn borers and corn earworms which can cause extensive damage to sweet corn. MVP, Bt and Dipel are safe choices you can use on your sweet corn to combat the bugs. Sevin is a chemical insecticide which will also do the trick. I usually don't dust unless I think the problem is particularly severe, which it usually isn't.

There is nothing like growing—and eating—sweet corn. Even if you don't grow it every year you should give it a try. Then fire up the barbecue.

CUCUMBERS

Cucumbers grow best in hot, dry places. Oversized pickup trucks driven by people with Mexican accents—and wearing big straw hats—can be seen traveling the highways in early spring heading **to** processing plants in the Midwest. The folks who drive these trucks probably never heard of places with names like Copper Harbor, Michigan, Duluth, Minnesota or Skowhegan, Maine.

We'll probably never see cucumbers hauled by the truckload out of the North Country. But it doesn't mean we can't grow plenty of cukes to satisfy our summer palates and to pickle for the winter months.

The northern region isn't ideal for growing cucumbers. However, like many edibles we successfully grow in the colder climates, we need only choose our seed carefully and learn a few tricks to be successful at this venture.

Fortunately, most varieties of cucumbers don't require many days to mature. Even Straight Eights, that old stand-

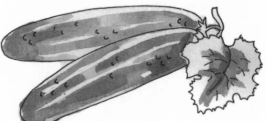

by sold in the supermarket, requires only 66 days to mature and grows well in the northern tier states.

However, cucumbers do need—and this is a must—good warm soil for germination. Thus, if you're sowing directly into your garden, wait until the weather is warm and settled before planting. You can increase the temperature of your growing medium by laying black plastic over it a few days before planting. Another method that will put the heat on fledgling cukes is to plant them under a floating row cover. I've had excellent results getting cucumbers started this way.

You can get a head start germinating cucumbers by placing them between two wet paper towels where it's warm. Or, you can simply soak them overnight before you plant. Either method will improve germination and get you off to a good start.

Insects can be a real problem for the young plants. I've gone away for a couple of days after my cucumber plants have come up and are looking healthy only to observe they've "disappeared" when I've returned. I've yet to identify the culprit. Unfortunately, it's difficult to dust the tiny plants with an insecticide. Floating row covers are an excellent way to protect young plants from the critters.

Cucumbers can be planted in rows or in hills much like you would squash or watermelon. Either way, you may want to mix in some well rotted manure or compost prior to planting. When I plant in rows I space my seeds about four to six inches apart in the row. That way I can afford to lose a few plants to the bugs. Likewise, when planting in hills, plant several seeds to a hill to allow for a possible disappearing act. The seeds should be sown about an inch deep.

When leaves begin to appear on the plants and it looks like the insects are going to spare them, pluck away all but 3 or 4 of the healthiest plants in the hill or thin to about one plant every eight inches in the rows. This will give the plants a better chance to flower and bear fruit.

Many folks start cucumbers inside then transplant into the garden around the first of June. These people tend to have cucumbers sooner than their neighbors. Sow the seed in cell type containers or peat pots about three to four weeks

before all danger of frost is past. Plants grown in peat pots can be set directly into the garden pot and all, thus sparing transplant shock.

Bush varieties are ideal for gardeners with limited space. Another way to save space is to train your cukes to climb a trellis or fence. Or you can grow them along (but not too close) to the south side of your sweet corn, allowing the vines to spread into the corn patch.

There are several varieties of cucumbers suitable for short season areas including these slicers: Jazzer, Supersett and Marketmore. Northern Pickling, Conquest and Miss Pickler will give you all the cucumbers you'll need for candy or dill pickles.

We may never head south with a truck load of cucumbers, but if done right, we could easily head to the farmer's market with a wheelbarrow full!

DILL

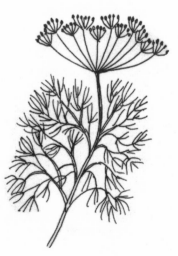

My wife and I were surprised the year we planted dill along the south side of our sweet corn. It not only thrived in that spot but the wide heads looked impressive swaying in the August breeze. We were also surprised to see we were the only ones to offer it at the farmer's market that year. It was a great seller!

Dill should be started from seed rather early in the spring. This will allow it to be harvested at the same time you harvest your cucumbers. Plant dill about a half inch deep in a clump or rows. Dill doesn't require a lot of thinning and is virtually free of insect problems. However, it takes a long time to germinate, so be patient.

This European herb is at its prime flavor when used freshly cut, just prior to going to seed (it can also be used after it goes to seed). The popular use for dill, of course, is for pickling. It can also be used to flavor salads and other dishes.

Hang the heads up in a dry place, like the rafters in your cellar or basement, and you'll have dill indefinitely.

ETTUCE

There's nothing like tossing just picked radishes, cucumber and cherry tomatoes into a bowl of fresh cut lettuce; top this with bacon bits and you've got a mouth watering salad that will go with any meal.

However, I must admit I have a problem with lettuce.

You see, lettuce generally flourishes in this country, resulting in—well—lots of lettuce. However, lettuce doesn't keep very long and you can't just leave it in the garden because it turns bitter quickly, especially during hot, dry weather. Thus, a lot of lettuce goes to waste around our house.

I shared my pessimism about lettuce with my northern neighbors. They promptly set me straight about this salad maker. Most said the best way to manage lettuce is to avoid over planting and by successive planting. The nice thing about lettuce is it can be initially planted very early in the spring and sown successively every ten days until the end of June. However, you have to keep it picked as it ripens so it doesn't bolt.

There are two popular types of lettuce: leaf and head lettuce. I've had luck growing both kinds including Black Seeded Simpson (leaf lettuce) and a miniature

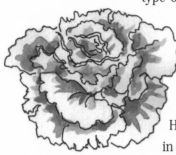

type of head lettuce called Tom Thumb. Other varieties suitable for the North include Iceberg, Buttercrunch, and a slow to bolt variety called Little Gem. Leaf lettuce and some short season head lettuce varieties, such as the Black Seeded Simpson, can be sown directly into the garden. However, head lettuce is generally started indoors or in a greenhouse and later transplanted outdoors.

Lettuce is shade tolerant. So if you have a shady spot in your garden, or want to plant something on the north side of your corn, lettuce is a good choice. In fact, it actually grows better in partial shade.

This is one vegetable insects haven't quite figured out. Cut worms are about the only pest that bother lettuce; however, they rarely cause extensive leaf damage.

My northern comrades had another thing to say to me regarding lettuce, by golly. "If you've seen the price of lettuce in the supermarket, you'd keep your lettuce picked!"

Geez, I'm sorry I bad mouthed this one.

ELONS

Growing cantaloupe in the North is about as practical as snowshoeing in Florida. Yet, while Floridians have probably never been on snowshoes, northerners have been successful—on occasion—growing melons.

If you can grow one of these sweet things, you'll not only have a tasty vittle, you'll have the bragging rights to go along with it! So let's get serious about growing melons.

Here's where an imagination comes in handy. As with most difficult-to-grow-in-the-North-veggies, seed selection is of utmost importance. Varieties worth a try in this country include Minnesota Midget, Hybrid Alaska, Sweet Granite and Flyer.

Start the plants from seed indoors during the last week of April or first week of May. Plant in peat pots which can be set into the garden pot and all, thus avoiding shock to the delicate root system. It's also important to harden off the young plants before transplanting in the garden. Start by setting the plants outside during the day for a couple hours, then three hours, four etc. until they've been out all night. Keep your plants protected from those harsh northwest winds which are common well into June.

Before setting melon plants in the garden, I dig a hole and fill it with a well rotted nitrogen-rich organic fertilizer, much like I do with my squash and pumpkin. However, the hole should be a tad shallower than that for pumpkin.

The folks from the Cornell Cooperative Extension in Voorheesville, New York, recommend using a row cover to get melons started. A fabric row cover will increase the daytime temperatures under the cover while warding off the bugs. This will give this delicacy a much needed boost. Be sure to remove the cover before the plant blossoms to allow for pollination.

Feed your plants generously at two or three week intervals with an all purpose fertilizer (like 12-12-12) or organic plant food. When your melons get as large as a tennis ball place them on metal cans so they're off the ground. This will draw a little warmth to the developing melon and allow the melon to ripen evenly and quicker.

Like I said, use your imagination. Try some other ways to get the young plants going including surrounding the melon plant with black plastic, which will draw more warmth into the plant (and ward off weeds). You may even want to combine this method with growing melons in a raised bed.

Hybrid Alaska Cantaloupe

Other methods worth trying include glass cloches and hot caps. Be sure to remove these or provide good air circulation during hot weather. I usually remove these season extenders around the first of July. By then I figure my plants are ready to go it alone.

Most folks don't have that much time to fuss with plants. However, with this one you'll have to give it a little extra attention. It will be well worth the effort.

ONIONS

Here's another vegetable special to folks who garden in frigid climates. Onions really do well in the North, especially in a sandy loam or humus rich growing medium.

Onions can be started by seed or from onion sets. Most northern gardeners plant onion sets. The growing season isn't long enough to start them outdoors from seed. Grocery stores usually stock the inexpensive sets in the spring. Choose from yellow Ebenezer, white Spanish and red hamburger onions. Plant by simply placing the little bulb in a furrow and covering it with about an inch and a half of soil. Compost can be added right into the furrow prior to planting.

Onion sets can be started quite early. I generally start my sets by the middle of May, depending on the weather. Some area gardeners get them in even earlier. Don't sweat the frost—onions can take it.

You can start eating onions any time after the stem appears above the ground. Just be careful the plant doesn't go to seed. This sometimes happens with onion sets. Should they set seed, the bulb on the bottom will become stunted and tough. To avoid this problem simply cut or bend back the seed pod when it takes on the shape of a nuclear reactor plant.

When the tops turn brown, it's time to harvest. I usually try to harvest before we get those all day rains we're accustomed to in the fall. It's important to pull the onions before the tops die completely. If the onion should sprout a second stem it will ruin the bulb for storage.

Onions require thorough drying. I usually place all my onions on a screen. Every few days I turn the onions so they dry thoroughly. When they've dried to my satisfaction I gather them up and place them in an onion bag. The bag is in turn hung by the bottom of a steel beam in my crawl space. Check your onions periodically during the winter to ensure no spoilage is taking place.

Like beets, onions don't need the help of expensive chemical sprays, enjoying as they do, a relative bug and disease free existence. A little fertilizer or manure tea during the summer should be sufficient to grow a fairly large "hamburger" onion.

ARSNIPS

Parsnips are nutritious and grow well in a sandy or sandy loam type soil. They tend to do poorly in heavy clay type soils. One remedy for this problem (which works with carrots as well) is to add some well rotted manure right into the row where you'll be planting your parsnips.

Parsnip seeds are sown like carrots, that is, about 1/4 of an inch below the surface of the soil and lightly patted with soft dirt. And like carrots, they take a long time to germinate. Some gardeners plant radishes along with the parsnips to mark the row and to help loosen the soil around the parsnips.

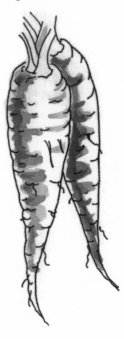

Parsnips store a little better than do carrots. You can dig them up in the fall after a good frost (the frost sweetens them) and store them in your root cellar, or simply leave them in the ground all winter. The latter method may require that you mulch them with a thick layer of old hay or straw. Dig them early in the spring but don't wait too long to eat them.

There are few problems experienced with parsnips and quite frankly they're not real popular so few varieties exist on the market. Two that I've run across are All American Parsnip and Lancer.

PEAS

As my daughters approached the house with their pockets bulging and grinning from ear to ear my wife was a little suspicious.

"OK, what's going on?" she asked.

"We picked some peas, Mommy," they replied. They were as happy as bears in a blueberry patch with their bounty.

I grew up near a pea processing plant surrounded by fertile farm land so it was common to eat peas right off the vine. My buddies and I would sit on the street curb and eat peas until we turned green. So when the peas are ready around my place I'm usually one step ahead of my children getting to the pea patch.

Peas are the first green thing I see poking out of the ground in the spring. It's a welcome sight after a long, white winter. Sweet peas can be planted as soon as the ground can be worked in the spring. Sow seeds one inch deep, leaving about 18 inches between the rows. You may wish to plant different varieties keeping in mind the "days to maturity." By staggering the harvest this way, you can eat peas all summer long!

The neat thing about peas is although the northern gardener may be limited in growing, for instance, different corn varieties, the field is wide open with peas. In other words, we can successfully grow just about any variety we choose. Moreover, peas love a cool wet climate, making them a sure bet in the North.

There are three types of peas: the low bush type that grow to less than two feet high; the climbers, that require support of some type, and snow peas. The latter are eaten pods and all and are excellent in stir fry and vegetable entrees.

Peas take up considerable space in the garden. You'll need about a 100 foot row of peas for a few dinners and canning and freezing. Marvel and Laxton Progress #9 are two space saving varieties which produce a generous quantity of peas. These are compact bush varieties which don't require staking.

Insects pose no problems for peas; however, watch for mildew. Cultivate well between the rows and support the vines with stakes and string, if necessary. One problem I've encountered with peas is weeds intermingling with the pea vines. It's pretty tough to get at these weeds once the peas have wrapped themselves around them. I usually wait until I've harvested my peas then raise the platform on my lawn mower and shave the whole mess down (do this before the weeds have a chance to set seed). Peas are a good "green manure" crop and should be worked back into the garden or heaped onto a compost pile.

Green Arrow is a popular variety across the country and does real well in the cold climate zones. However, they do require staking. Other peas worth experimenting with include Maestro, Bounty, Knight and Daybreak.

PEPPERS

This heat loving plant makes me shiver every time I think about growing it. Peppers do **much** better closer to the equator. Some may even say they have no business being grown in the northern states. Which isn't exactly true. Thanks to the work of scientists and savvy seed savers, there are several varieties which do quite well in the North. However, like tomatoes, you'll need to get this one down to a science if you want to be picking sweet peppers at summer's end.

Plant peppers inside about eight weeks before the last frost. Peppers will need warmth and artificial lighting to get a good start indoors. Or, you can buy quality transplants from a local nursery. Folks in Nova Scotia have luck with a variety known as Earliest Red sweet pepper. Other short season do-gooders to look for are Northstar, King of the North and Ace.

Peppers are very sensitive to frost and cool weather so plan accordingly. Harden off your plants by setting them outside for a couple of hours at a time each day, gradually increasing the time spent outside until they can be left out all night. Transplant into the garden when the weather is warm and settled. Use hotcaps or sawed-off plastic jugs the first few weeks to increase the heat and provide wind protection. Be careful, however, that you don't burn your plants with the hotcaps or plastic milk jugs. This can be avoided by cutting out a "tent door" (these doors are provided with hotcaps) for ventilation.

Hot peppers actually do as well or better than sweet peppers in the cold climates. Varieties to choose from include Hungarian Hot Wax, Ring of Fire and Canape Hybrid. And don't forget Grandpa's Home Pepper which will produce up to 50 mild peppers per plant.

As the plants grow taller, try a trick I learned from a neighbor. Circle the plants with an 18 inch high wire fencing or chicken wire like I've suggested for tomatoes. Then take a black garbage bag and fit it over the fencing. Now cut out the top of the bag to allow for air and rain to enter. This will provide wind protection and draw the heat this plant so badly craves.

You'll need to coax this cold blooded vegetable along with a little fertilizer of some type. Miracle Grow or an organic fertilizer can be applied early in the year. Side dress with an all purpose 12-12-12 or manure tea at two week intervals up until the plants blossom.

I have to admit frustration with peppers; although I'm not sure if it's the peppers or the summers (or me?) I blame the most. The last couple of summers I've looked on sadly at my stunted peppers while hovering over them in my flannel shirt. Perhaps I should have lent the shirt to the pepper plants!

Experiment with a few varieties to see which one(s) appeal to you and your particular climate. Pay particular attention to the "days to maturity" indicated on the packet and the hardiness zone to ensure you're growing peppers suitable to the area.

POTATOES

The potato is to the Upper Midwest and Northeast what the orange is to Florida. What makes the potato so at home in these regions is its relative tolerance to cool weather and its ability to thrive in acidic soil. Post-glacial coniferous growth and decay has resulted in a predominantly acidic soil type throughout the North which potatoes love. Our typically sandy-loam soil also makes potatoes a good inhabitant of this region.

Northerners take pride in growing potatoes much like our southern neighbors pride themselves growing juicy red tomatoes. Unfortunately, we don't see too many red ripe tomatoes in this country. However, it's not unusual to see lush, bushy potato plants—in flowery purple bloom—swaying in an August breeze. Beneath these plants grow delicious red and white potatoes.

Potatoes are relatively easy to grow. Prepare a spot in the garden by cultivating the soil well. Initially, fertilize with a super phosphate fertilizer. You can side dress later with a complete fertilizer, such as 12-12-12. Go easy on the organic material, such as compost and manure. As a rule, the older and drier the better. Also, don't dump in any lime or wood ashes into your potato bed. Potatoes will become "scabby" if the pH is too high. An ideal pH for potatoes is between 5.0 and 6.0.

Potatoes grow well in the author's sandy loam soil near the St. Mary's River near Sault Ste. Marie in Michigan's Upper Peninsula.

Potatoes can be planted in mounds or in rows. I plant mine in rows to maximize garden space. This works well for me. I leave enough room between rows to run my roto-tiller down through.

Work the soil well before planting. I use seed potatoes and left over spuds from the previous year. Some folks are skeptical about using "kitchen" potatoes because if they are hybrid potatoes, they won't re-seed. I've never experienced this problem. Perhaps I'm just lucky. However, I must admit treated seed potatoes tend to germinate better than do the kitchen potatoes.

Either way, I slice my seed potatoes with a kitchen knife prior to planting. I leave a couple of potato "eyes" on each section that is cut away. I do this a couple days before planting so they have time to dry and heal over.

For row planting, dig a trench 3-4 inches deep and place the cubed potato in the trench, cut side down. Space these 6-8 inches apart. Cover and firmly pack with about an inch of top soil. You can also plant potatoes in mounds or hills much like you would squash and pumpkin. Space four or five potato eyes around the mound. These mounds should be spaced about 18 inches to two feet apart

depending on whether you want to run a cultivator between the mounds. Planting in mounds is necessary for folks who garden in wet, low-lying areas.

When the plants start to appear above the ground cover them lightly with soil. This will protect them from frost and give you a start on hilling your plants. When the plant reappears through the soil and the danger of frost is past, continue to hill around the plants. If you don't hill your plants the potatoes will become exposed to the sun, causing them to turn green and develop a poisonous layer called solanine. If this occurs you can cut away the green areas before you prepare them for a meal.

There's nothing like "new" potatoes in the middle of the summer, boiled and served with a little salt and pepper, butter and topped with chopped parsley. However, to pick potatoes to store in your root cellar or crawl space, wait until the vines die away completely in the fall—after a couple of frosts—then dig them up. Children like to help with this chore.

There are a number of potato varieties to choose from; Norland and Kennebec are the most popular in the North—the former for its delicious flavor, the latter for its suitability for baking and ability to keep over the winter. Other varieties include Red Pontiac, an early red spud, Russet Burbank (excellent for storing), Superior and Yukon Gold.

PUMPKINS

Along the shores of Lake Michigan near Escanaba, Michigan and the so-called "Banana Belt" they grow pumpkins like Hawaiians grow coconuts. But closer to Lake Superior and many other locations in the North, it's a little more difficult.

But not impossible.

Bush Spirit Pumpkins make good jack-o-lanterns and take up minimal space in the garden.

In fact, over the past dozen years or so I've had plenty of pumpkins for my children's jack-o-lanterns and a few to share with the elementary school for their fall carnival.

Seed selection is critical if you want to grow mature jack-o-lanterns consistently in this country. However, you could be daring like the man who planted a Big Max pumpkin seed in a gully on his property near Marquette, Michigan. The last I heard it was over 60 inches in diameter (it could still be growing for all I know!).

If you want ripe pumpkins year after year I suggest you plant a bush variety such as Hybrid Spirit Bush or Autumn Gold. These varieties require less than 90 days to maturity (compared to over 100 for Big Max and Connecticut Field) and take up a lot less space in the garden; both can be grown for pies or carving.

Start by digging a hole two feet deep and about three feet wide. Then toss about three shovels of well rotted sheep, horse or chicken manure into the hole. At

North Country Gardening

by Neil Moran

this time you can also spread a handful of a complete inorganic fertilizer around the hole. Lastly, fill the hole back in and form a mound over the top.

Now you're ready to plant. It's a good idea to plant several seeds in a hill to ensure that four or five plants come up. I usually space eight or ten seeds around the mound and push them into the soft dirt with my finger, about a half inch below the surface. I then sprinkle dirt into the crater I've made with my finger and pat it firmly with the palm of my hand (incidentally, kids like to help with this aspect of gardening).

Sow pumpkin seed directly into the garden no later than the last week of May. The first leaves will usually appear before the last frost so be sure to cover the plants as needed. After the first plants begin to appear check to see which ones look the best and pluck all but two plants from the hill. These will be the plants you'll want to baby the rest of the summer.

Pumpkins are big eaters and will require plenty of fertilizer. I like to use a complete fertilizer (10-10-10) to side dress my pumpkins throughout the summer.

When the plants are up and well established I sprinkle a handful of fertilizer in a circle about six to eight inches from the base of the plant. You can feed your developing plants with an all purpose granular fertilizer or a little Miracle Grow at this stage. About three weeks later sprinkle another handful of fertilizer around the drip line of the plant. Be careful not to over-fertilize; this will cause the leaves to turn brown and slow the growth of the plant.

By now your pumpkin plants should be starting to bush out (Hybrid Spirit Bush and Autumn Gold are fairly compact plants and won't run along the ground like some varieties). Fertilizer should continue to be applied throughout the summer at three week intervals right up until the plant blossoms. You can also water during dry spells to encourage the growth you'll need so they'll ripen by the end of the summer.

Eventually, it will be difficult to apply the fertilizer close to the roots due to all the plant growth that is in your way, but do the best you can. Fortunately, by now the roots are obtaining nutrients from the manure and fertilizer you've buried beneath it.

Quite frankly, I hold my breath each year hoping the pumpkins will mature before we get a hard frost. But lo and behold they usually make it before Jack Frost hits my jack-o-lanterns. If they don't turn orange, I make sure my pumpkins get picked and placed in the barn or other shelter before we get a severe frost. Pumpkins won't keep well after being clobbered by a hard frost.

If they don't all turn orange before the killing frost, don't despair. They'll turn orange in plenty of time for Halloween, especially if you bring them inside a couple of weeks before Halloween. Set them next to the wood stove and they'll turn orange before you can say "Booo!"

RHUBARB

Rhubarb should be called the "Napoleon of the North Country." Although it is small in stature, this member of the buckwheat family is hardy. It can withstand any confrontation with this frigid climate and still come out victorious!

Purchase rhubarb root stock in the spring at a local nursery or order from a seed catalog—or better yet, snatch some of your neighbor's rhubarb. This way you'll be assured of having a hardy root stock for your area. Rhubarb roots can be halved or even quartered to grow all the rhubarb you'll ever need. Dig a hole about a foot deep and fill it about half way up with well rotted manure or compost. Cover this with about two inches of soil then stick your rhubarb roots in the ground, covering the roots with only about 2-4 inches of soil.

You won't harvest any stalks the first year. However, you'll be rewarded for your work when you see the plant begin to emerge and even proliferate by summer's end. Fertilize during the course of the summer with a little 12-12-12 or manure tea.

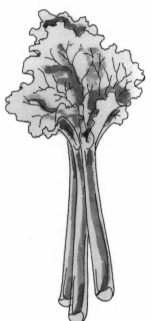

Look out the following spring! You'll have enough rhubarb to pucker up the whole neighborhood! Keep the stalks pruned back so they don't go to seed and you'll have rhubarb all summer. Rhubarb is excellent for making jam and pies; it freezes well also.

Rhubarb should be ordered from seed catalogs in February or March to get here on time to plant in the spring while it is still cool and wet. Choose from Chipman's Canada Red, Crimson Red and Victoria.

RUTABAGAS

There is a curious culinary novelty unique to the Upper Peninsula of Michigan. It is, quite simply, a meat and vegetable stew wrapped tightly in a flour crust and baked in the oven. Back in the 1800's the miners who worked in the copper and iron ore mines in towns with names like Copper Harbor and Iron Mountain stuck these meals in their lunch boxes and descended into the mines. When the lunch whistle blew, these meals were still warm.

These meals are called pasties and they're incomplete if they don't include chopped rutabagas mixed in with the meat, potatoes, carrots and onions (it's more than a coincidence all these vegetables grow well in the Upper Peninsula).

Pasties are still popular today. Tourists like them as much as the locals. In fact, these days they're sold in fast food joints so you can grab one from your car window and head for the mines . . . or school or office!

Rutabagas grow well in a sandy loam soil in cooler climates. They can also be started in heavier clay type soil, particularly if you mix a little organic matter right into the rows.

Though not as appreciated as corn and tomatoes, rutabagas are a sure bet to grow to maturity in this region, growing well into the fall. And they store well in a cool, humid environment. If stored properly (around 40 degrees is ideal) they will

provide good nutritious eating all winter. I keep my "bagies" in a crawl space under the house; we've had tasty rutabagas right into April.

You don't need to plant rutabagas early. An early sowing of rutabagas will produce a root the size of a basketball (well, almost) by early September. I usually plant mine no sooner than June 1. You may also try succession planting. In the southern climates, gardeners plant a spring crop they harvest in late July, then a fall crop that's harvested in about October. I compromise and plant the first week of June, which gives me plenty of time to grow a nice sized rutabaga.

Rutabagas are planted much like carrots. The tiny seeds are sprinkled into a shallow furrow, then covered with about a quarter of an inch of fine topsoil and patted firm with the palm of the hand. When they reach about an inch or two high, start thinning them back. Thin gradually until the plants are from six to eight inches apart.

Insects will sometimes feed on the tops of rutabagas without causing any damage to the root. A light dusting of rotenone or Dipel should take care of this problem. Or, if you're like I am you won't worry about it unless the tops show signs of becoming severely infested with bugs. The only other pest worth mentioning is the slugs which cling to the root. These can be avoided by regular cultivation

between the rows. A little lime sprinkled around the roots and worked in well will also help alleviate your slug problems.

The most common variety of rutabaga (and one of the few) is the Purple Top. This type grows quite large if given the chance. And if picked after the first hard frost it will bring delight to any pasty lover, whether it be miner or tourist.

SPINACH

A steady diet of spinach throughout the summer should help us make it through the long, cold winter. Spinach is a good source of vitamins A, B, C and iron. If we could only get our kids to eat it . . .

Spinach can be sown as transplants or directly into the ground. Either way, start it early as it favors cool weather. Or plant successively up until late June. Perhaps our cool, wet summers in the North are one advantage we have over our southern neighbors (who wants all that heat anyway!).

Plant spinach in rows about two feet apart. When the plants form four or five leaves, clip these right down to the stem. This will encourage a second edible growth and prevent the plant from "bolting," or going to seed. Spinach is excellent

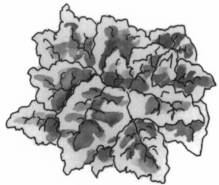

either cooked or tossed as a salad with a vinegar dressing and bacon bits. Salad made from spinach leaves is a specialty in many restaurants these days.

Early varieties of spinach include Olympia and Melody. Imperial Sun (hybrid) and Imperial Express varieties can be planted for a spring or fall harvest.

SQUASH

There's nothing I find more challenging than raising squash. Squash, like children, needs to be nurtured along until it's big and strong and ready to pick. A lot of folks in our neck of the woods wouldn't venture to grow squash (even though they've raised lots of kids!). Yet I've had bushels of luck growing hubbards, acorns and buttercup squash.

Careful seed selection will get you off on the right foot. Pay attention to the number of growing days required for each variety. If possible, select squash varieties with less than 85 days to maturity.

Northerners are somewhat limited in their choice of squash. I've had luck with Hybrid Early Acorn (75 days) and Table Ace (75 days). I have to admit defeat on several occasions with butternut squash, which is actually my favorite. Trouble is, there just aren't many short season varieties of butternut squash to choose from.

Summer squash is quite a bit easier to grow. Varieties include Black Magic Zucchini, Yellow Crookneck and Straightnecks. In fact, many folks grow an over abundance of these. Summer squash doesn't store well and you can only eat so much squash.

Squash generally loses more than it gains if transplanted from pots into the ground. That's why I wait until the weather is settled and the ground is warm (usually the last week of May or first week of June) and sow my seed directly into the garden. If my squash comes up before the last frost I can always cover it. I can also use hot caps and row covers during this period to help them along. I've found row covers work exceptionally well in "jump starting" squash and other vine crops. These can be left on until the plants start to creep along the ground. Remove the

covers before the plants blossom to allow for pollination. Also, make sure bugs can't get in around the bottom of the covers, which can be detrimental to your plants.

Plant in mounds about 4-6 feet apart, depending on the variety you choose. It's also best to plant in an area where the vines can spread should they really take off (which they should if you follow these directions).

I follow the same mound preparation method for squash as I do for pumpkins (see culture on pumpkins). That is, I dig a two foot deep hole beneath my mound and dump in some well rotted manure that the plant can tap into later in the season.

Sink several seeds into the mound. Cool, wet days in June can make germination tricky. That's why I sow about eight seeds per mound to ensure I get a few plants. Also, it doesn't hurt to soak the seeds overnight in warm water to hasten germination. When the plants grow to three or four inches high thin back to two plants—spaced several inches apart—on the mound. Then get ready to pamper them.

I feed my squash throughout the summer with generous helpings of water, fertilizer, and mulches. The rewards come when the plant starts to take on a life of its own. I enjoy taking people out to the garden to show off my squash as it spreads outside the borders of my garden.

Squash plants are big feeders. I usually side dress the plants starting in late June with a 12-12-12 fertilizer. I feed my plants every two weeks until the plant blooms. However, be careful not to over fertilize. Too much nitrogen can result in a lot of plant growth and very little fruit production. Another way to feed squash is with a manure tea.

I also surround my plants with well rotted barn manure, extending about three feet away from the base of the plant. Mulching will keep down the weeds,

trap moisture underneath and allow nutrients to seep down into the soil and around the roots.

As the dog days of August approach, the few that we have in these parts, squash blossoms should brighten up your day. It's a harbinger of what is to follow. Now you can step back and let nature do the rest; your part is done. Next thing you know you'll be giving birth to a five pound squash!

The nice thing about winter squash is it stores well in a cool, dry place. Try the thumb test to find out which will be the best keepers. If your thumb easily pokes through the skin of a squash it's best to eat that one right away or put it towards the front of your pile in the storage bin.

Like children, squash needs a lot of patience and attention to grow to maturity without driving you nuts worrying along the way!

TOMATOES

Growing a vine ripe tomato in the North Country is quite a challenge. Perhaps that what's make us northerners tough (besides coping with the long, hard winters). I've risen to the challenge on a few occasions, offering as it be, a little advice to share with the reader.

Now when I refer to growing vine-ripe tomatoes I'm talking from the perspective of someone who doesn't have a lot of time to fuss for the final product. Besides, one should learn the basic tomato growing culture before experimenting with the various gimmicks we've devised to beat mother nature.

Shopping for the right tomato is half the fun. Lately, I've restricted my tomato shopping to Johnny's Selected Seeds. Johnny's extra early varieties include GEM State and Sub-Arctic Plenty. Folks as far north as Alaska have reported having

North Country Gardening

North Country Gardeners will do anything for a red ripe tomato. This Sault Ste. Marie resident devotes a greenhouse exclusively to growing the "Elusive One."

good luck with these varieties. Gardeners in the Upper Peninsula of Michigan have had considerable luck with Kotlas and Oregon Spring. All these varieties require less than 60 days to maturity. They'll produce tomatoes ranging from 2-6 ounces.

If you've tried them all and still haven't had any luck consider these Siberian varieties (if these don't grow in the northern United States, which ones will?): Sash's Altai and Zaryanka. These varieties are offered by High Altitude Gardens out of Ketchum, Idaho. These two can cope with the cooler temperatures better than most tomato varieties. And they'll produce a red ripe tomato quicker than any of the southern varieties.

Consider determinate and indeterminate varieties when purchasing tomato seeds or plants. An indeterminate will need staking and bear a lot of fruit. A determinate doesn't need staking. The latter grow closer to the ground which can cause insects to gather around the fruit. Experiment with both types to determine which one is right for you.

by Neil Moran

Start tomato seeds in a soil-free peat starting mix 6-8 weeks before the last frost. The room temperature for starting seeds should be between 70 and 80 degrees at all times. When plants reach 2-3 inches tall separate by transplanting to a larger container.

It's important at this stage not to let the plants grow tall and leggy. This can be avoided by suspending a shop light 2-3 inches from your plants and leave it on for about 16 hours each day. Another way to grow strong-stemmed tomato plants that can withstand our often brutal spring winds, is to rub the tops of plants from time to time while they are under the shop light. Research on tomatoes has pretty much confirmed that this technique works.

The next step is to harden off the plants (or move them to a greenhouse if you have one). When temperatures reach at least 55 degrees outdoors place them in a sunny, sheltered location (be sure they're protected from the stiff winds which can start up anytime during the day). Bring them in at night. Do this for a couple of days before setting them out in the garden.

Here's the critical part. Tomatoes should be planted when the weather has settled considerably. In reality, the weather is hardly ever "settled" in late spring in this harsh climate. The "ol' northwesters" can be almost as wicked in early June as they are in November. More times than I care to remember I've set out healthy plants in June only to watch them bend and twist—and sometimes break—in the wind. Don't be in too big of a hurry to set your plants outside. Besides, tomatoes need temperatures above 55 degrees for growth to occur.

When you do set your tomatoes out, (which you'll invariably have to do), you may want to consider planting them in trenches, especially if you're planting a lot of tomatoes. Dig a 4-5 inch deep trench with a hoe then lay the tomato in the trench, slightly bent over away from the prevailing winds. Bury the roots, leaving the rest of the plant at an angle close to the ground. This method will lessen the

impact of those stiff spring breezes. The plant will eventually straighten itself up as the weather settles and the plant begins to establish itself.

You can also construct or purchase various windbreaks to coax your plants along. One method is to place two bales of hay at right angles to a third bale and place the plant inside. This works well as a wind block, however it does require considerable fussing, especially if you need to hunt down some bales of hay. Wall-o-waters also work well. These can be purchased from seed and nursery catalogs. Water is filled in the surrounding walls, which will release warmth to the plant at night while providing protection from the damaging winds during the day.

A neighbor shared this tomato growing secret with me: find some old fencing (18-24 inches high) and surround your tomato plants like you would for an indeterminate tomato. Then take a black trash bag and insert it upside down over the outside perimeter of the circular trellis. The bottom is then cut out which becomes the top. This relatively fuss-free device should provide all the wind protection and extra warmth your plants need. I'm amazed at the difference this has made with my plants. Tomato plants started this way seem to run a couple of weeks ahead of the ones which aren't afforded this luxury.

Tomatoes will benefit from an application of phosphorous, but be careful with the nitrogen. Too much nitrogen will result in a lot of plant growth and little fruit. I usually mulch plants with well rotted manure; this will not only keep the soil warm and moist but will offer the slow release of nutrients from the manure.

If the plants make it through June without too much trouble you should be on your way. By now your mouth is watering for that first juicy red tomato slice to put between your bacon and lettuce when all of sudden—beetle bugs! A mosquito with a hard shell. Make sure you have some bug dope on hand when the various garden pests make their appearance. Rotenone will discourage the flea beetle. Other bugs to look out for are tomato hornworms, potato beetles and aphids.

Also, protect your plants against mildew by clipping off all but the main stem of the plants. This will allow badly needed aeration, especially during prolonged rainy weather.

The heartbreak we so often experience with tomatoes is they get nice and big but fail to ripen. If this is the case there are a couple of ripening methods you can try. One method is to grab hold of the bottom of the plant by the stem and give it a sharp pull, in effect, disturbing the roots. The other method is to take a pointed shovel and dig down around the plant, effectively slicing the roots of the plants. Both methods operate under the premise that if you disturb the root system it stops the growth of the plant and energy will go into ripening the fruit. And of course, you can always pick the green tomatoes and place them in the window (however, this is really not necessary because tomatoes will turn red anywhere where it is warm).

So if you ignore conventional wisdom and make a quest for red ripe tomatoes remember to obtain as much information about this elusive red fruit (or is it a vegetable?) as you can.

ATERMELON

Watermelon is underrated among northern gardeners. No, we can't grow the humongous ones that leave us breathless after we lower them into a grocery cart. But we can grow petite watermelons—"icebox" varieties that actually fit in your refrigerator. And though small in stature, they're humongous in flavor!

Start watermelons inside about the first week in May in a nonsoil potting mixture, such as Pro-mix. I like to start my watermelon in peat pots which can be later set directly into the garden without disturbing the root system. Melon seeds need temperatures hovering around 75 to 80 degrees fahrenheit to germinate properly. Try to time your indoor planting so the plants will be 3-4 inches tall when the danger of frost is past.

Gradually harden off the young plants before transplanting into the garden. Hardening is accomplished by placing the plants outside for a few hours each day before planting them directly into the garden.

Watermelon plants should be spaced 6 to 8 inches apart atop a small mound. Space the mounds at least 2 feet apart. Unlike the supermarket varieties, icebox melons need minimal space to grow. Instead of producing one huge melon, these plants produce three to five small melons (5 to 12 pounds each) per vine.

Sugar Baby is my favorite and has produced vine ripe melons most years. There are other varieties well worth the effort (and challenge) such as Sweet Favorite (a little larger red fleshed melon that ripens after Sugar Baby) and Garden Baby.

Yellow fleshed varieties are elbowing their way into the gardens and palates of icebox watermelon lovers. Some folks even prefer the yellow to the red fleshed, claiming they taste like pineapple. Johnny's Selected Seeds out of Albany Maine offers a variety called Sunshine which they claim is the "best yellow fleshed watermelon." These need 75 days of good growing weather to mature in comparison to the 65 days Henry Field's Hybrid Yellow Doll requires.

Here are a few things you can do to grow melons successfully:

• Order the right seeds. It's absolutely necessary to choose varieties that grow well in the cold climate zones (see "Sources for Seeds and Equipment").

• Place black plastic around the plants. This method will increase the temperatures around the root of the plant and get them off to a good start.

- Feed generously. Watermelon thrives on nitrogen and phosphorous. Many folks rely on organic products to provide these nutrients. Well rotted chicken or sheep manure is a good choice. The gradual leaching of nutrients into the soil will help feed your plants all summer. Sea Mix (a 3-2-2 mixture of fish emulsion and seaweed) can also be used and is applied mid-season to give them that necessary boost. And of course, you can side dress with an inorganic fertilizer such as 12-12-12.

- Use row covers. My watermelons get quite a jump on the season if I leave a row cover on for two or three weeks at the beginning of the season. Be sure to remove them before the plant flowers to allow for pollination.

Now it's late August and your tongue is wagging as your icebox watermelons begin to show signs of ripening. When do you pick it? The usual method is to wrap on it with your knuckles to see if it *sounds* ripe—kind of like knocking on your neighbor's door. This isn't always the most reliable way to tell if it's ripe. A better way is to watch for a creamy yellow substance on the surface of the melon and a brown, withered tendril on the vine where the fruit is attached. If it's ripe it will break away from the stem with ease.

So if you thought growing a ripe watermelon in the North Country was out of the question, you have another think coming. Plant some of these mouthwatering varieties, then get ready to enjoy a true summer delight.

REFERENCES FOR VEGETABLE CULTURE SECTION

—*A Sierra Club Naturalist's Guide*, by Glenda Daniel and Jerry Sullivan, Sierra Club Books, San Francisco, 1981.

—*Dial-U*, Insect and Plant Information, University of Minnesota.

—*Down-to-Earth Vegetable Gardening Know-How* by Dick Raymond, Garden Way Publishing, 1975.

—*Eco Gardening*, Department of Fruit and Vegetable Science, Cornell Cooperative Extension, Fact Sheet #6, Spring 1993, Wolfe, David; Pritts, Marvin; Eames-Sheavly, Marcia; Albany County, Voorheesvill, New York 12186-0497.

—*Gardens Alive!* Vol. 11, No. 4, Insect Guide.

—*Grow "Icebox" Watermelon*, by Vicki Mattern. Organic Gardening, April 1993.

—*Johnny's Selected Seeds*, Summer 1994 Catalog.

—*Lettuce Lessons*, Connie Fitz, National Gardening, Vol. 10 No. 3. March 1987.

—*The Green Thumb Book of Fruit and Vegetable Gardening* by George Abraham. Prentice-Hall Inc. Englewood Cliffs New Jersey 1970.

RAMBLES

ASPBERRIES

Raspberries are a favorite of gardeners everywhere. They are easy to start from nursery stock and don't flower until after the last frost, thus eliminating the risk of crop loss.

Some retail stores acquire raspberry plants from suppliers far south of us. If you take the time to look closely the bargain you think you're getting is rated for zone 5 or 6. Bargain berries **can** be had at discount stores, but it's best to pay attention to the hardiness zone indicated for each plant.

A better bet is to purchase raspberry plants from a reputable nursery in the area. These plants are much more apt to do well in our hardiness zone (zones 3 and 4). You can also get hardy native stock from friends and neighbors. Raspberry plants tend to multiply over the years and some folks are happy to share these plants with you just to get them out of the yard.

Hardy red raspberries include Boyne, Cambry and Chief.

Planting Raspberries

Plant raspberries in the early spring so the plant has a chance to properly establish itself before winter. Fall plantings can result in poor growth and subsequent winter kill to the plants, especially here in the North. Be careful when you order raspberries and other live plants from seed and nursery catalogs; they tend to ship these before the frost is out of the ground. It's best to attach a note to your order telling them when you want them shipped. In zones 3 and 4 it's usually no earlier than late April.

Plant raspberries about four inches deep, spacing them 3 feet apart in the row. Rows should be four or five feet apart. Water the new plants well, however don't fertilize new plants with a commercial fertilizer.

Once the plants are established (usually the following year), you can apply a layer of sawdust or wood chips. This will increase fruit size and yield. Ammonium nitrate or an all purpose (12-12-12) fertilizer is recommended for developing plants. Apply at the rate of two ounces per plant just about the time the plant is budding in the spring. Be sure to spread this two or three feet away from the plant.

Raspberries prefer a light sandy-loam soil but will grow in clay types as long as it's well drained. Like asparagus, you should mix in a healthy quantity of well rotted compost and manure into the ground before planting.

Pruning

Raspberry canes live a short life. They grow one year, produce fruit the next, then die off. These canes can be cut at ground level and discarded. The remaining canes can be pruned at hip level, and staked if necessary before winter sets in. Also, look for dead or dying canes which can also be eliminated. With a little pruning and annual feeding you can enjoy raspberries for many years.

RAPES

If you're afraid to prune plants, then don't grow grapes. Grapes need to be trained on a trellis and kept pruned back to four strong canes to have any chance of surviving—and producing grapes—in this climate. The good news is once you learn to prune grapes properly you're practically assured of having grapes each year.

North Country Gardening
by Neil Moran

The next bit of advice is to select hardy stock and plant in a sheltered area in your yard. I recently planted a Beta grape in a south facing corner of the yard, protected by a grove of trees to the north and a building to the east. Quite frankly, I was once skeptical of growing grapes this far north. However, my Beta grape vine has made me a believer.

Choosing Hardy Grapes

Grace Wurster, owner of Timbercrest Garden Center in Marquette, Michigan, has wintered over several different varieties of grapes (and other plants) which she sells to her customers. In my opinion, anyone who winters over their plant stock in the North has confidence in these varieties. Grace also has over 49 years in the business.

Thus, I'm confident the Beta grape she sold me will do well over in this frigid climate where I live, as long as I take care of it. Grace and husband Roland sell most hardy grape varieties except Concord, which Roland claims doesn't do very well in these parts.

Grace and her husband have never shared my skepticism with grapes. Roland said they do well in their area. Marquette sits right on Lake Superior and is somewhat protected by the northwest winds that normally blow off the lake. Perhaps it's the warming effect of the lake i.e., the micro climate, which plays a role in this success.

Be sure to pay attention to hardiness zones and such when choosing grapes. Gurney's Seed & Nursery Company rates their Beta grapes to zone 4-8. They claim this is their hardiest grape. Miller Nursery in Canandaigua, New York offers tried and tested varieties for the region including Seibel and Hardy Worden grapes. Other hardy varieties include Valiant, Foch and Bluebell.

Folks in northern Wisconsin have concluded that French hybrid grapes and seedless cultivars won't do well in their neck of the woods. I'm sure this holds true for many areas of the North.

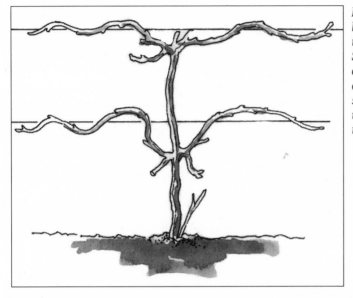

It's imperative that you keep your grapes pruned if you want grapes. Select 4 canes and cut out the rest as shown above. This diagram also shows how to place the vines on a trellis (note the horizontal lines).

Planting Grapes

As previously mentioned, plant grapes in a sheltered area in your yard. Add a little organic matter into the planting site. Grapes will occupy a spot for over 30 years. It's also preferable to plant in the spring so the plant can establish itself before winter. Apply a thick layer of mulch around the base of the plant before winter.

You'll need to start training your grapes soon after they send out shoots or vines. Roland recommends placing two cedar posts 8 ft. apart (with the plant in the middle) and make a trellis with three strands of #9 wire spaced two feet apart. The shoots will gradually climb the trellis as you train them to spread out along each ascending strand.

Grapes need annual pruning. Roland clips back all but the three "eyes" on each shoot. He said he once offered to help a neighbor do his pruning in this manner. The neighbor was a little disappointed with the mess Roland left behind, but the man didn't mind after he finally got to eat grapes! The nursery man said after this lesson the man was able (and willing) to do his own pruning.

STRAWBERRIES

Fresh strawberries are a treat for gardeners everywhere. They are relatively easy to grow in cold climate zones. In fact, they prefer cool, moist days over hot, dry ones. However, extremes of either can cause low yields of berries.

Here again, we should select hardy disease resistant stock from a reputable nursery to get off to a good start with strawberries. A lot of time and money is wasted purchasing plants unsuitable to the region or of poor quality.

Choosing Your Plants

Once established, early bearing strawberries should provide the home gardener with a crop of tasty berries by the end of June or first part of July. Early bearing strawberries that have performed well in the North include Earliglow, Crimson King, Premier, Catskill and Sparkle.

There are many everbearing cutivars on the market. However, be careful. Fort Laramie is one of the few everbearing varieties which has done well in this region. Generally speaking, our season is too short to grow everbearing strawberries. If you insist on giving them a try you can also choose from Ogallala, Ozark Beauty and Quinault.

Preparing a Site

If you don't have time to keep a berry patch clean of weeds you may wish to post-

pone growing strawberries until retirement. Weeds can definitely be a problem. However, there are a few tricks that help hold back the weeds so you can have the experience of growing your own sweet, fresh and delicious strawberries.

Effective weed control invariably starts prior to planting. Prepare a site by cultivating the year before with a rototiller, if possible. Combine this method with raking out the clumps of quackgrass and removing them from the bed. Another method would be to kill off the vegetation with an herbicide such as RoundUp, then work the ground well with a roto-tiller. The bed would then be ready to plant the following year.

A third method, recommended if planting near a building or isolated spot in your yard, is to cut away the sod with a spade or fork and remove the entire sod. Then build the bed back up with a mixture of top soil, well rotted compost and manure or potting soil.

Planting Time

Strawberries should never be planted in a raised bed due to the possibility of winterkill. Strawberries need a good layer of snow to make it through the winter. Avoid planting where the wind sweeps the snow away or an icy crust forms over your bed. Most hardy varieties winter quite well in the North providing they're insulated well with snow.

There are two ways to plant strawberries: matted and in hills. The matted method requires you set the plants 18 to 24 inches apart in rows three feet apart. With this method the runners are trained to fill the area between the rows. With the hill method the plants are set in slightly raised mounds 15 to 18 inches apart in rows 3-4 feet apart. The difference between the matted and hill method is with the latter method the runners are clipped back. This will cause the plant to grow upward and bushy. Regardless of what method you use, lay a thick layer of straw, newspaper or even cardboard between the rows to discourage the weeds.

Be sure new plants are watered well to get off to a good start. Strawberries are shallow growing plants so they need a lot of water to not only establish themselves but to produce mouth watering strawberries. Strawberry plants are heavy

feeders. A combination of manure tea and a good sheep or horse manure will adequately feed a patch of strawberries. A complete fertilizer can also be used.

Protection From the Elements

Strawberries have a tendency to bloom early if the weather is nice, thus becoming susceptible to spring frosts. Our late spring frosts can definitely detour our plans for shortcake. Thus, it's a good idea when you mulch in the fall to leave it on until after the hard frosts in the spring. This will keep the ground cool and delay blooming. You may also consider late bloomers (and late bearing) varieties such as Albritton, Jerseybelle, Marlate, Redstar, and Sparkle. All these have performed well in the North.

You can provide yourself with a little peace of mind over the winter by mulching your strawberry plants with straw, evergreen boughs or shredded bark before the snow flies. As mentioned before, a good layer of white stuff provides the best protection; you may even wish to shovel a little extra on your plants to ensure adequate insulation from the cold.

SOURCES FOR BRAMBLES

(Strawberries, Grapes and Raspberries)

Home Fruit Cultivars for Northern Wisconsin, University of Wisconsin-Extension, B.R. Smith & T.R. Roper, Madison, Wisconsin.

The Green Thumb Book of Fruit and Vegetable Gardening, By George Abraham, Prentice-Hall Inc. Englewood Cliffs, New Jersey, 1970.

Cold Climate Gardening, by Lewis Hill, Garden Way Publishing, 1987.

OVERWINTERING YOUR VEGETABLES

You reap what you sow, store what you reap and eat what you store. Folks who don't share our love for gardening find this too labor intensive (except for the eating!).

Winter storage is the icing on the cake for the home gardener. You've pampered and toiled over your fruits and vegetables all summer; now it's time to put them up for the winter. If done right, you'll have tasty, nutritious produce until the next harvest.

Compared to canning and freezing, storing produce can involve a lot of work—initially—but less work in the long run. First, you have to dry your vegetables. Root crops and tubers, such as carrots, onions, rutabagas and potatoes, can be dried by spreading them out and turning them each day so they dry thoroughly. I spread mine out on the garage floor on a sheet of plywood and turn them with a broom, dusting off the dirt as I turn them. I watch for produce which may be starting to spoil as I do this. The drying will take about a week.

Storing Produce

Different fruits and vegetables require different temperatures for storage. Root crops, such as carrots, onions and potatoes, store best close to the freezing point, while vine crops and green vegetables, such as squash and cabbage, store best around 45 to 55 degrees fahrenheit.

Note that temperatures vary around the inside of a storage bin. Warmer temperatures can usually be found near the top of the structure, while it's cooler towards the bottom and in the corners. Store produce accordingly.

Root crops and fruit can be placed in the storage bin in boxes or slatted crates. However, these crops will store better if you spread them out on shelves or a dry floor. I wrap my cabbage tightly in newspaper which allows them to keep a little longer. Green tomatoes can be stored in a similar fashion, although the temperature needs to be at least 50 degrees. Check tomatoes every other day for spoilage. Tomatoes can only be stored in this fashion for less than a month.

Check all the produce in your storage bin for spoilage every other week or so. As soon as you notice produce becoming soft, pitch it into the compost pile.

Another method worth trying, though I admit I haven't, is the carrots-in-a-garbage-can trick. Fill the bottom of the can with about four inches of sawdust. Add layers of carrots and sawdust to the top of the can. Cover with a lid and store in a cool place. Some garden books suggest digging a hole and placing the can in the hole. I doubt this will work in the far reaches of the North. The "permafrost" is sure to penetrate the barrel and spell curtains for your carrots. I'd suggest storing the can of carrots in an attached garage, well house or outbuilding.

Dried beans, such as Jacob's cattle beans, store quite well anywhere it's dry and around 55 degrees. After the leaves on the vines die off, pluck the plant and all and allow to hang for several days in a dry attic or even a garage. Once the beans are completely dry and have been thrashed, they can be stored in a jar in the pantry.

Onions dry best when placed on a suspended screen for about a week. They can then be stored in a relatively warm place (45-55 degrees) for most of the winter with very little risk of spoilage. Incidentally, white onions store better than yellow onions. I've stored white onions, suspended from the beams in my crawl space, for over six months with minimal spoilage.

Do it Yourself Storage Bin

Modern dwellings generally have heated basements, though the basements in some of the older homes are still rather chilly. If you have a cool corner in the basement, commonly the northwest corner, you can build a vegetable storage bin that will keep the warm air **out**.

This will make an ideal storage bin in an already heated basement. Keep the light out. Ventilation will help reduce spoilage.

Construct a wooden enclosure to the desired length and width and insulate throughout with fiberglass or styrofoam insulation. Build shelves in the bin to stack your produce. A light is ideal to see your way around the bin and periodically inspect produce for spoilage. Include a door that can be latched closed. A vented window will allow for air circulation. You can also keep the door ajar to allow for air flow.

Inside temperatures should range from just above freezing to less than 60 degrees fahrenheit. Maintain humidity at 80-90% for root crops. You may need to add a humidifier to achieve this level of humidity.

Tips for Storing Vegetables

Vegetable	Location	Ideal Temp.	Length of Time
Beans (dry)	Cool, dry room	32°F-40°F	Indefinitely
Cabbage	Crawl space, cellar	near 32°F	Late fall to winter
Carrots	Crawl space, cellar	near 32°F	Fall to winter
Cauliflower	Storage cellar, crawl space	near 32°F	4-6 weeks
Onions	Cool, dry space	32°F-40°F	Fall to winter
Parsnips	In garden, crawl space	near 32°F	Fall to winter
Potatoes	Crawl space, storage cellar	35°F-40°F	Fall to winter
Pumpkins & Squash	Cool basement, storage cellar	55°F	Fall to winter
Tomatoes (green)	Warm basement	55°F-70°F	4-5 weeks

Canning and Freezing Produce

Canning vegetables is more work in the long run than storing. There are two ways to preserve produce using the canning method. One way is the water bath method, the other is with a pressure cooker. Both methods will produce mouth watering vegetables you can store for the long winter ahead.

High acid fruits and vegetables like pears and tomatoes can be canned using the water bath method. Low acid vegetables, which include beans, beets and carrots, must be processed in a pressure cooker.

The spread of bacteria and other micro-organisms can be avoided by using only fresh, high quality fruits and vegetables from the garden. Botulism is a deadly derivative of bacteria. Its development can be prevented, however, by processing low acid foods in a pressure cooker. Also, be sure to sterilize all jars, lids and utensils in boiling water prior to using them.

There is one problem I've run into relating to our cool climate and canning. Some summers it can be downright cold in late August when I'm canning my garden vegetables. The cold air in the kitchen has prevented some of my jars from sealing properly. My hunch is that the jars cool too rapidly for them to properly seal. In fact, I've found if I eliminate drafts in the kitchen by closing doors and windows, that most of my lids will seal properly.

Always check the center of the lids with your thumb before you store them away. If the lid goes down when you press it with your thumb, that jar is not sealed properly and should be used right away. Also, try to store produce in a dark, cool (less than 70 degrees fahrenheit) place.

Some people prefer freezing vegetables over canning. Freezing requires less fussing in the long run than does canning, mostly because you don't have to spend time sterilizing jars and lids. Studies show, however, that freezing is more expensive than canning (storing vegetables is the cheapest method of all).

Most vegetables can be frozen by the blanching or steaming method. The exception to this is tomatoes and vegetables that lose their crispness, such as cucumbers, radishes and celery. Lettuce doesn't freeze real well, however spinach will by using the steaming method.

The freezing point for produce is zero degrees. It's a good idea to clean out your freezer prior to freezing your fresh produce. This will provide good airflow. Bags and packages of produce should also be stored in such a way as to leave about an inch between each package, if possible.

It's important to freeze produce as quickly as possible after it has been picked. Enzymes go to work immediately after produce is off the vine to induce spoilage. Even after produce is frozen, this spoilage continues, only at a slower pace.

Try to be practical about what you freeze. Fruits and vegetables will only maintain their superior quality for a limited time after being froze. Resist doing what my wife and I have done in the past, that is, freeze literally everything we could get our hands on, only to have it go to waste due to spoilage and freezer burn.

North Country Gardening

by Neil Moran

Regardless whether you choose to can or freeze your produce, be sure that you use vegetables at their peak period of flavor and freshness. Or like my mother used to say: "I'll get the water boiling, you go pick the sweet corn."

Refer to the references at the end of this chapter for specific information on canning, freezing and storing vegetables.

REFERENCES

Better Homes and Gardens New Cookbook, Better Homes and Gardens, Des Moines, Iowa.

Canning, Freezing, Storing Garden Produce, United States Department of Agriculture Information Bulletin 410, December, 1977.

Down-to-Earth Vegetable Gardening Know-How by Dick Raymond. Garden Way Publishing, 1975.

Speed Pressure Cooker and Canner, General Mills Inc.

BEAUTY IN THE NORTH

Nothing beats the winter blahs better than the thought of the colorful array of flowers that await us in the spring. And if we've planned our flower beds and borders carefully we should see some color before the snow leaves the woods.

There is such a variety of flowers to choose from and ways to plant them that the beginning gardener can become confused to the point of throwing in the garden trowel. Should I prepare beds or borders? Plant annuals or perennials? Which varieties are suitable for my particular area?

This section is not intended to be an all inclusive guide to growing flowers. The possibilities for flower gardening are infinite. Books abound on this subject which range from the practical to poetic (see recommended reading at the end of this section).

The following pages will give you some firm ground to stand on when making plans to include flowers in your landscaping plans. They will help the northern gardener sift through the multitude of floral offerings to come up with varieties best suited for their region. Because here in the North we're looking for flowers that will give us the biggest "bang for our buck" in terms of the time we have to enjoy them before the snow flies again.

Seed and Plant Selection

It's imperative that we take time to learn which flowers will do well in the cold climates. Examine the catalogs that arrive in your mailbox, particularly those from nurseries that grow their stock in the northern states. For instance, Johnny's Selected Seeds test their stock in Albion, Maine. They also make flower seed selection simple by indicating if a variety is a hardy or tender annual, perennial or biennial.

Be careful when you purchase seeds or plants at a supermarket or retail store unless you're **sure** they will do well in this region. Quite frankly, you can't go wrong with petunias, pansies and hardy geraniums. These flowers are hardy for the region. However, you'll be wasting your money trying to grow southern belles this far north. Refer to the flowers listed at the end of this section before you go bargain hunting, whether it be at a retail store or professional nursery.

If you take the time to select the right catalogs and examine different plants for degree of hardiness and adaptability to cool climates, it will be time well spent. You'll be on your way to growing beautiful beds and borders.

Preparation

Whether you've decided on flower beds or borders (or both), preparation for planting will be your biggest job you'll be faced with. Because there is only one technique I've found that really takes care of the stubborn quackgrass ground cover rhizomes—remove them.

Slice down through the sod along the perimeter of your future garden site with a spade or garden fork. Next, cut away individual sections to the size you feel you can handle. It's best to remove as much top soil from the root systems as possible. Either shake out the dirt with your hands or loosen it up with a small garden fork. Toss what's left in a wheelbarrow and haul it away. This stuff is heavy, so don't bite off more than you can chew (or lift).

When you've removed all of the sod from your planting site build the soil level back up to avoid leaving a sink hole for water to collect in. Back fill with good sandy loam soil from another part of your garden. You can also dump in some (extremely) well rotted compost and manure (sheep manure that is at least ten years old is virtually all humus and can be mixed into the existing top soil to build it back up). The more convenient, albeit expensive way to fill in a bed or border, is to replace the sod with a mixture of potting soil, top soil and sphagnum peat moss purchased at a nursery or retail store.

Flower Beds

Beds are usually placed in the center of a lawn and attract attention to that area, consequently taking a little away from the hedges and borders in a yard. In addition, they gobble up the center of a yard, eliminating the possibility of recreation in that area. Some folks may also see beds (and this is definitely in the eye of the beholder) as making a small lawn look cramped.

Of course, you can make a bed as large or small as you wish. For instance, some folks like to plant a flower bed in a small lawn with pansies, dwarf marigolds and some late blooming asters. Larger beds can easily handle coneflowers, daylilies and even peonies.

In contrast, borders are usually located adjacent or along side buildings, sidewalks, fences or woods. Northerners create beautiful borders by planting tulips and daffodils, which flower early, followed by annuals such as petunias, cosmos and zinnias which flower most of the summer. These can be punctuated with perennials such as yarrow, dianthus and baby's breath which will bloom at different times during the growing season, providing the homeowner and passerby with breathtaking beauty and color throughout the season.

Flower Borders

Borders can turn a dull, snaking sidewalk into an experience of natural color and splendor. This walkway can be lined with petite annual flowers such as dwarf marigolds, petunias, and sweet alyssum. If the eye were to follow the curve of the sidewalk and end up in front of the house, it would observe the taller plants: dahlias, foxgloves and lupine.

This far north, it's especially important to plant borders in areas that get at least partial sun during the day. Avoid borders along north facing buildings which not only receive minimal sunlight, but take a long time for the ice and snow to thaw in the spring. These areas would be particularly poor for growing herbs and perennials.

North Country Gardening

by Neil Moran

Annuals

The nice thing about annuals is they generally hold their blossom much longer than do perennials.

Annuals can be started indoors in April or May in a non-soil medium such as you would use for vegetables (see Starting From Seed). You'll need a good warm place to germinate the seed and a sunny south facing window or grow light to continue their growth.

Some annuals are hardier than others. The northern green thumb is sometimes in a bit of a hurry to put out flats of flowers around the yard at the first sign of warm weather. Be patient. It will

Ruth and Curt Johnson harvesting flowers in Bayfield, Wisconsin. These will be dried and sold at the Johnson's shop in Cornucopia.

only result in a lot of wasted effort (and money) if you plant a couple hundred flowers only to have them snuffed out by frost a few nights later. Unfortunately, in this country we've got to keep an eye out for frost well into June. Cosmos, marigolds and zinnias are all tender annuals which won't tolerate even a light frost.

My wife keeps a step ahead of frosts by planting a small circle of tender annuals in a bird bath. She can set these out in the front lawn early; in the event of a frost all she has to do is carry the bird bath into the garage. She is patient enough to wait until the second week of June before she plants the rest of her tender annuals around her water pond and in her beds and borders. Planting a few annuals in a portable bed like this is another way we can extend the season with flowers. And by starting out the season with just a few annuals, we avoid the work and

130

headache involved with covering a whole flower bed with blankets when the meteorologist says "chance of frost this evening."

Another method of extending the season with annuals in this area is to plant a few in a border near a house or building. Attach a roll of plastic sheeting about two feet above the border to your house or outbuilding. This sheeting can be conveniently unrolled and draped over the annuals as needed.

Some annuals, such as sunflowers and sweet alyssum, are much hardier than zinnias, marigolds and cosmos. They can be started ahead of some of the others and will hold their blossom longer at the end of the season. A good strategy is to plant hardy annuals as early as you can (after the daffodils have lost their bloom), then follow up with tender annuals after the danger of frost has passed.

Many a beginning gardener (myself included) has fallen into the trap of growing too many flowers in too little space. It's hard to envision, in the early spring, that the underdeveloped flowers you're transplanting or the bulbs you bury will actually grow into bushy, beautiful plants. In the process they can become crowded and take on a cramped appearance to the onlooker.

Both annuals and perennials require some forethought in regard to spacing and location. Some flowers need full sun and wind protection to reach maturity, particularly in the frigid climates. And of course, some grow small, some grow tall and others bush out or climb on trellises, fences or decks; and they come in all different colors! These are all things to consider prior to planting flowers. Fortunately, this can all be handled by getting to know the flowers you're planting, by reading detailed descriptions in books and seed catalogs and by plotting out your garden beforehand on paper. Northern gardeners know that's why God made such long winters!

Perennials

Perennial gardening dates back several centuries. It first gained prominence in 19th Century England, but saw a slight decline when annuals were introduced to Europe. Now, it appears to be blossoming again in England and America as gardeners everywhere realize the beauty and satisfaction of growing perennials.

North Country Gardening
by Neil Moran

In the North, some folks shy away from growing perennials, according to Nancy McDonald, editor of The American Cottage Gardener magazine. Yet Nancy grows more than 1700 species and cultivars of perennials in her 22 beds in Grand Marais, Michigan.

There's a distinct advantage to planting perennials. Once you've planted perennials you're pretty much done with them; they'll come up year after year. You'll still need to weed and feed your hungry plants, but you have to do that with annuals as well.

Another advantage of perennials is different kinds can be planted in a variety of soil types. Certain perennials can be planted in ditches, sandy hillsides and other areas that would be otherwise bare or filled with noxious weeds. Groundcovers such as hen and chickens and ivy are good choices for these areas.

Perennials can be started from seed, according to McDonald. She said some are no more difficult to grow than carrots. However, like any other plant, some need to be started indoors, in advance of the growing season.

Perennial plants can be expensive to purchase. However, you'll find that once you get that insatiable diet for planting perennials (it really is habit forming) you'll run into veteran perennial planters who are more than willing to share their flowers with you as they thin their own perennial beds and borders. And like any other shopping, you can find quality plants at reasonable prices by shopping around either by mail order or at a nursery. Also, watch your local paper for perennial swaps whereby locals get together on a Saturday and swap plants.

Cottage Gardening

The English were famous for the cottage garden design, although they didn't call it that at first. They simply mixed different perennials, annuals, fruit trees, vegetables, herbs and shrubs into an area and stood back and observed what happened. What usually happened was beautiful to behold as the daffodils, tulips, roses, and apple trees bloomed at random all summer. English cottages were literally surrounded by plants, hence the name cottage gardening.

This cottage garden is reminiscent of an old English Cottage garden.

During the Victorian Era, these freewheeling gardens gave way to the excruciatingly organized annual beds. The affluent folk of the day were impressed by the exotic annuals that arrived from far off places. And they were equally impressed at how they bloomed all summer. This type of design can still be seen in city parks, surrounding public buildings and in many of our friends' and neighbors' floral gardens.

Perennials returned to prominence by the late 19th Century. Leading the way in this movement were English gardeners William Robinson and Gertrude Jekyll. They argued against the "wasteful" use of annuals which were destroyed at the end of the season. They also deemed annuals "unnatural"; they had no business in a "real gardener's" flower patch.

Apparently, perennial and annual flower lovers compromised because most cottage gardeners today include both kinds of flowers along with herbs, small shrubs, vegetables and fruit trees.

Ira and Nancy McDonald kneel by one of their 22 cottage garden beds in front of their Grand Marais, Michigan, home.

Winter Care

Most folks worry about what will happen to their bulbs and plants over the winter. And for good reason. The memory is still frozen in our minds of the winter of 1994 when the average temperature for two straight months (January and February) was 0 degrees fahrenheit here in the Upper Peninsula of Michigan. Many days went below zero including a few that dipped to -35 F. Folks who were responsible for thawing frozen pipes claimed the frostline sunk to six feet!

This unusual cold snap and relative lack of snow depth had a detrimental effect on plants. Throughout the summer of 1994 I heard horror stories of established fruit trees, roses and hardwood trees succumbing to the elements. Surprisingly, perennial flowers and herbs seemed to survive better than the larger plants.

It's important, then, to select your planting site carefully. Avoid planting where the wind sweeps the snow away; also, avoid planting in extremely wet areas. The roots of plants need warmth in the spring to get going. If they're sitting in clay under water it'll be pretty hard for them to get warm. One way to provide drainage and extra warmth to flowers, especially where clay is predominant, is to plant in a raised bed. If possible, bring in some good topsoil to raise it up. Surround the raised bed with treated landscaping timbers or old railroad ties. This will provide good drainage and also allow the soil to warm up quicker in early spring.

Another way to winterize our flowers is to provide three to six inches of a good mulch over our bulbs and plants. Do this just before winter. This will protect against heaving which can kill a plant. One choice for a good mulch is well rotted manure mixed with hay or straw. This will protect the roots from the harmful effects of the frost. A good blanket of snow over this should provide our plants with protection and us with peace of mind over the winter.

Leaves and grass clippings will also protect perennials, especially against heaving, which is particularly evident where there's minimal snow cover. Another way to protect flowers is to lay pine boughs at right angles to each other over the dormant plants.

Feeding Flowers

There are several ways you can feed hungry plants. A little water soluble fertilizer, such as Miracle Grow, will get your pansies, asters and other annuals off and running in the spring. It can also give a boost to sickly looking plants. However, if you have good, organically maintained soil you shouldn't need to rely on commercial fertilizer.

One thing about our cool, wet summers is we seldom experience drought. And some folks, like Ruth Johnson, who dries and sells flowers in Bayfield, Wisconsin, say our flowers appear deeper and richer in color due to the abundance of rain and snowfall in the North, in addition to the cool breezes off the Great Lakes. Relative lack of sun may also play a role as flowers can become bleached by constant exposure to the sun.

Perennials need a spring and early summer feeding of 5-10-5 or a strong manure tea. Healthy summer growth will help them winter over better. Be sure to avoid fall feeding; the plant needs to prepare to go dormant in the autumn. Bulbs do well with an application or two of bone meal at planting time and again each spring.

Pests

One of the most common garden pests in this region (besides deer) is the slug. Our cool nights and generally mild (as opposed to hot and dry) days are well suited for propagating slugs. Slugs are a particular problem on flowers with wide, leafy foliage such as hosta, delphinium and campanula.

The chapter titled "Coping With Critters" introduces you to a dozen or so non-chemical but lethal strategies for dealing with slugs and other pests. One old standby method to deal with slugs is the beer-in-a-jar-lid trick. The slugs will crawl in this and drown. Another is to lay a board flat on the ground near the slug infested area. Check it the following morning. You should find lots of slugs that can be destroyed by the method of your choice. Avoid chemical slug repellents which are allegedly toxic to birds and other small animals.

Deer are another threat to our beautiful flowers. They will eat virtually any type of flower. Deer are particularly troublesome to residents who live in close proximity to the woods, with no open fields in between. About the only thing you can do to put a stop to this intruder is by fencing in your yard, which of course, is expensive.

Wildflowers

Wildflowers may be just the answer to adding color and beauty to an otherwise drab meadow, or perhaps, to get out of some mowing.

Either way, you don't need an ideal soil type to grow wildflowers. However, seed selection is important. Beware of the variety packs that promise the moon. These packets usually contain seeds for flowers, such as rosebud orchids, which don't have a prayer in our neck of the woods. Johnny's Selected Seeds offers packets of wildflower seed called Northern Mix that is formulated especially for us folks in the North (see *Sources for Seeds and Equipment* section).

And don't be seduced by the notion, as displayed on wildflower packets, that you can simply spread some seed across a fallow area and Presto!, you've got wildflowers. Quite the contrary. In fact, preparing a site to sow wildflowers is hard work mainly because the sod needs to be removed or tilled under prior to planting. Large areas can be plowed and disced with a tractor. If planting in an old pasture or meadow, burn the old hay before working the soil.

The problem with preparing the soil in the spring is you would really have to hustle to get the new ground worked up and everything planted and still have time left over for your other garden chores. Thus, you may want to try to make time in the late summer and early fall for this task.

Once you've removed the top soil you're ready to plant. Start by doing some shallow roto-tilling. This will turn over the moisture in the soil which will help germinate the seed. Broadcast the seed (not too thickly) immediately following the roto-tilling.

Next, use a water-filled lawn roller to press the seed into the damp soil. This will not only help the seed germinate but will prevent it from blowing away in the wind. I've had excellent results applying this method when planting wildflowers and lawn cover seed.

There's no need to water wildflower seed if it's already relatively wet. Of course, it won't hurt, especially right after the seed is sown.

Despite the initial work, an area chock full of annuals and perennials is a sight to behold. It will provide years of beauty with little to no maintenance each year. It's also an excellent way to convert a difficult lawn area or otherwise drab section of property into something attractive, at a relatively low price.

• • •

Below are just a few of the tried and tested perennial and annual flowers you can choose from to plant in your beds and borders. This list is by no means exhaustive.

Perennial Flowers for the Region

Balloonflower (platycodon grandiflorum)

Bellflower (campanula)

Black-eyed Susan (rudbeckia)

Catmint (nepeta)

Columbines (aquilegia)

Common garden peony (paeonia lactiflora)

Common wormwood (artemisia absinthium)

Coral bells (heuchera sanguinea)

Cottage pinks (dianthus plumarius)

Creeping phlox (phlox stolonifera)

Daylilies (hemerocallis)

Dwarf or cushion asters (aster dumosum)

Evening primrose (oenothera)

False spirea (astilbe x arendsii)

Hardy or true geraniums (geranium)

Heartleaf bergenia (bergenia cordifolia)

Hen and chickens (sempervivum)

Hosta (plantain lily)

Japanese primrose (primula japonica)

Lady's mantle (alchemilla)

Lilies (lilium)

Lupine (lupinus)

Marsh marigold (caltha palustris)

Oriental poppies (papaver orientale)

Perennial salvia (salvia x superba)

Phlox (phlox maculata and paniculata)

Potentilla (cinquefoil)

Purple coneflower (echinacea)

Red valerian (centranthus ruber)

Sedum (stonecrop)

Shasta daisies (chrysanthemum maximum)

Siberian iris (iris sibirica)

Speedwell (veronica spicata)

Tickweed (coreopsis)

Yarrow (achillea)

Annuals and Biennials For Northern Climates

Not all of the below listed flowers are true annuals, but are treated as annuals in the North, such as, snapdragons, pansies etc. Some of these will over winter.

Also, most of these have several cultivars, or varieties which gives the northern gardener plenty of flowers to choose from.

Annual baby's breath (gypsophila elegans)

Annual phlox (phlox drummondii)

Bachelor's button (centaurea cyanea)

Borage (borago officinalis)

California poppies (eschscholzia)

Chinese forget-me-nots (cynoglossum amabile)

Clarkia (clarkia)

Cosmos (cosmos)

Deptford pinks (dianthus armeria)

Dianthus (Telstar series)

Edging lobelia (lobelia erinus)

Foxgloves (digitalis)-biennial

Larkspur (consolida)

Love-in-a-mist (nigella)

Monkeyflower (mimulus x hybridus)

Painted tongue (salpiglossis sinuata)

Panicle larkspur (consolida regale)

Pansies and Johnny-jump-ups (viola x wittrockiana)

Pincushion flower (scabiosa atropurpurea)

Pot marigold (calendula)

Shirley poppies (papaver rhoeas)

Silver sage (salvia argentea)-biennial

Snapdragon (antirrhinum majus)

Stocks (matthiola)

Sweet alyssum (lobularia maritima)

Sweet rocket, dame's rocket (hesperis matronalis)-biennial

Sweet pea (lathyrus odoratus)

REFERENCES

Color With Annuals, Barbara Ferguson, Editor; Ortho Books, 1987.

All About Perennials, Ortho Books, A. Cort Sinnes, Michael D. The Creating Cottage Gardens, Mary Davis, Angus & Robinson, 1993.

Flowers for Northern Gardens, By Leon C. Snyder, 1983, University of Minnesota Press, Minneapolis.

From the Good Earth! Susan Price, Lake Superior Magazine, Vol. 16, Issue 4, September 1994.

Harrowsmith Perennial Garden, by Patrick Lima, 1987, Camden House, Ontario.

McDonald, Nancy, Editor of *American Cottage Gardener* magazine.

McKinley, Edited by Ken Burke 1981.

North Stars, by Shepherd Ogden; NATIONAL GARDENING Vol. 10, No. 12, December 1987.

Pictorial Guide to Perennials, M. Jane Coleman Helmer, Ph.D and Karla S. Decker, B.S. Merchants Publishing Co., Kalamazoo, MI 49001, 1991.

THE NORTHERN HERB GARDEN

Growing herbs in the cold climates requires patience and understanding. Though many herbs are quite hardy, they still require some nice weather, a commodity we can't seem to get enough of in these parts.

We can overcome this handicap by getting to know our herbs. Learn to differentiate between the hardy and tender herbs. The listing at the end of this section will save you a lot of time and money. Not only will you learn which herbs will do well in the North, but which ones are perennial, annual and biennial.

Getting Started With Herbs

The beginning herb grower should start with the easy-to-grow varieties. Parsley, sage, oregano, winter savory and chives do especially well in the North and can be readily used in the kitchen. It's best to start herbs from seeds inside or purchase plants from a nursery, according to herb grower Colleen Arbic, of La Galerie in Sault Ste. Marie. Arbic also recommends starting out small and enjoying some immediate success with herbs. As you gain experience and knowledge of the plants and plant culture you can easily expand your repertoire of herbs for your home garden. Also, acquire books on herbs and talk to experienced herb growers to get an idea what will grow best in your particular location.

Lavender and other perennial herbs tend to get off to a slow start in the Midwest and Northeast, especially in some of the mountainous regions of New Hampshire and Vermont. Lavender is one of several herbs that grow from the root up, thus it's easily assumed to be dead in spring, and is often mistakenly dug up. Thus, we need patience to allow these types of herbs to take off—which they will—in late May or early June.

To become acquainted with herbs, label them as you plant them in your herb garden. Plastic or wooden stakes are good ways to label herbs. Another way to keep track of what's planted is to draw a map. Indicate, at least roughly, the location of your various herbs and other plants that occupy your beds and borders. This can be done in the fall, which is also a good time to decide if you want to rearrange your herb garden. Arbic spends a little time each fall making notes on her maps indicating what may have looked out of place or too bushy the previous season.

Local nurseries provide the best bet for obtaining herbs hardy enough for the North. Most nursery folks will be glad to assist you in selecting herbs for your particular garden site (in terms of soil type and exposure to the elements). Nurseries, such as Johnny's Selected Seeds and Garden City Seeds—who test most of their seeds in the northern states—provide quality seeds as well as sound advice. You can also get good deals at discount stores if you know what you're looking for. You may wish to take along this book to help you select varieties suitable for your area.

Gardening books, especially those that address our southern neighbors, tend to give advice on flowering times and plant height irrelevant to us, due to our unique growing conditions. Experimentation is the rule here. This is where a garden journal comes in handy for logging flowering times and other notes you wish to keep.

For the would be herb gardener I've offered a variety of tried and tested herbs for this area. The veteran herb grower may even find a few here they've never previously considered. The joy of growing herbs is the informal network of herb growers who share the virtually endless treasure of garden lore surrounding herbs. Folks who meet and discuss herbs invariably leave with a new herb they've just got to try. Or perhaps they learn of a new use for an herb they've been growing for years.

A Brief History of Herbs

"And ye shall take a bunch of hyssop, and dip it in blood that is in the basin, and strike the lintel and the two side posts with the blood that is in the basin; and none of you shall go out of the door of his house until the morning."—Exodus 12:12.

by Neil Moran

A history of herbs could be nothing but brief in a book of this type. Herbs date back several centuries—before biblical times. The neat thing about herbs, from a historical and botanical standpoint, is we're growing essentially the same herbs as did the ancients. No gene swapping or other genetic engineering has tainted herbs.

Herbs have been used by virtually every culture for food, medicine, ornamental arrangements and to ward off the spirits. Barbara Barker, owner of Willow Grove Farm in Brimley, Michigan, believes herbs are the original plants given to man by God to remedy all of our ills. Barker is worried that the heavy use of synthetic pharmaceutical substances—in place of herbs—will result in a significant breakdown in the human immune system.

The use of herbs as medicine is legendary and continues to this day. Horehound, for instance, has been used for centuries to sooth sore throats: wormwood for fevers, borage to sooth inflammation and hyssop for colds and fevers.

Barker cautions against experimenting with herbs, especially for medicinal purposes. She contends that some of the older books list some herbs, such as pennyroyal, as safe for consumption, when in fact, it's poisonous. Monkshood, which grows wild throughout the Midwest, has pretty violet-blue flowers but is also poisonous. Native American warriors coated their arrows with this herb prior to battle.

What Barker and others suggest is to purchase herbal medicines and remedies from health food stores or pharmacies. In other words, it takes a professional to prepare herbs for medicinal purposes. Like mushroom hunting, picking the wrong herb for human consumption can be downright deadly!

As a food source there are common seasonings made from herbs: basil, dill and thyme, to name a few. Horseradish, a plant some folks don't recognize as an herb, is of course, a popular meat garnish. Lesser known edible herbs include borage (the stalks can be used like cucumber in a salad) anise (the seeds are used as a seasoning for salads, cakes and fish) and lovage, which can be used like celery. Lovage grows quite well in the frigid climates. However, it needs a lot of room to grow, thus it's not suitable for planting in a small herb garden or flower bed.

Mike and Tammy Rundell weed a bed of sage, one of several perennial herb beds at Willow Grove Farms in Brimley Michigan.

Soil, Location and Feeding

The nice thing about herbs is they can be grown in some difficult soil types and locations. They're found in heavy or sandy soils, growing between rocks, and in partially shaded areas. Experimentation is the rule here. Some herbs such as rosemary, tarragon and basil, require soil rich in humus and nutrients, while others such as evening primrose and chamomile can be grown in clay, sand and even gravel.

One thing all herbs require is good drainage. This can be a problem in low lying areas where clay is the predominant soil type. These soil types will require some generous applications of humus producing materials such as compost, grass clippings and well rotted manure. Or you can plant a raised bed above the clay. Fill a raised bed with a rich topsoil, purchased from a lawn and garden supply or from a contractor, mixed with well rotted compost and livestock manure.

Some herbs, such as chervil and angelica, actually require a location that is shaded part of the day. Others, such as anise, dill and coriander live for the sunshine and warmth. Herbs classified as tender annuals generally require sunny, protected locations, particularly if started early. One way we can grow some of the more exotic types of herbs in the North is to plant them on the south side of the house or a building where they get plenty of sun and are protected from the wind.

Herb beds should be treated like most any other garden plot. Soil should be tended to each season to create and maintain the humus rich environment which absorbs and holds moisture and nutrients. Mulches of grass clippings and leaves can be layered between herbs to help retain water and discourage weeds. Mulching will simultaneously add organic matter to your soil. Raised beds planted exclusively with herbs need refurbishing every few years. In fact, you may want to practice crop rotation by relocating some herbs to another bed. Livestock manure, leaves, grass and compost are all ways to amend over worked soil.

Herbs don't require inorganic fertilizers. In fact, nitrogen will encourage abnormal growth which results in an exaggerated need for water. Herbalists who dry herbs for later use would flinch at the suggestion of using inorganic fertilizers. Well rotted sheep or cow manure is an excellent organic source of fertilizer for herbs. If the odor of manure is of concern remember it need not be applied all at once, rather work it into the soil in small amounts each fall and/or spring. Seaweed and kelp are also good organic fertilizers which can be purchased commercially in nurseries. Another organic fertilizer I use is my home brewed "manure tea." Manure tea is a mixture of well rotted manure and rain water.

Extending the Season with Herbs

We can extend our season—and fascination—with herbs in a variety of ways. Herbs such as thyme, basil, and parsley can be started from seeds indoors anytime providing we've got the proper artificial lighting (see "Starting From Seed). The edible leaves of these plants can be clipped and used in the kitchen as needed. And they can eventually be transplanted to the garden by either planting the whole plant or dividing the roots.

We can also extend our appreciation of herbs in the fall when we dry herbs for tea, floral arrangements or fragrance. These herbs can be enjoyed all winter long. And finally, we can enjoy the taste of herbs all winter by mincing the leaves of edible herbs, such as basil and oregano, and placing them in the freezer in a plastic baggy.

We can continue to garden with herbs after the snow falls by bringing plants inside in the fall. The roots of rosemary, sage and thyme can be divided and wintered over in your windowsill. Although this can be messy and time consuming for the busy gardener, it is a way to enjoy watching herbs grow while the snow accumulates in your herb bed.

Herbs Voted Most Likely to Succeed in the North

KEY:

HA=Hardy Annual
P=Perennial
A=Annual
BI=Biennial

Angelica: (Angelica archangelica) (HA), requires moist, rich soil, partial shade, although it will do well in full sun in North. Used for cooking, potpourri and medicine. Average height: 4'.

Anise (Pimpinella anisum) (A), easy to grow for culinary, medicinal and cosmetic use. Average ht: 2'.

Artemisa: (Ornamental Silver Mound) (P), easy to grow for fresh or dried wreaths and arrangements. Average ht: 6" - 24."

Basil: (Oscimum basilicum) (A), requires rich soil and full sun. Also grows well as a potted plant. Popular spice for sauces but also used as a fly deterrent, potpourri and to produce cosmetics. Average ht: 18."

Borage: (Borago officinalis) (A), requires rich soil. Unique cucumber flavor is used to flavor salads. Also grown for its medicinal value. Average ht: 30."

Chamomile: (Matricaria recutita) (A), is grown for its use as a tea, medicine and for potpourri. Average ht. 18."

Chamomile: (Chamaemelum nobile) (P), makes a good hair rinse and ground cover. Average ht. 6."

Caraway: (Carum Carvi) (BI), seeds are used to flavor cakes, etc. Grows in good to moderate soil types. Average ht. 18." Seeds will appear the second year.

Catnip: (Nepeta cataria) (P), grows in good to moderate soil types. Used as a cat tonic, insect repellent, tea and cosmetics.

Chervil: (Anthriscus cerefolium) (HA), will tolerate shade or full sun in North. Culinary uses. Average ht. 24."

North Country Gardening

by Neil Moran

Chives: (Allium schoenoprasum) (P), easy to grow in most soil types. Onion flavor used in the kitchen. Flowers are used in fresh and dried arrangements. Average ht. 12."

Coriander: (Coriandrum sativum) (HA), grows in average soil type. Used for cooking and potpourri. Popular spice in Mexican food. Average ht. 24."

Costmary: (Chrysanthemum Balsamita) (P), won't blossom in shade. Used in the kitchen, for potpourri and cosmetics. Average ht. 36."

Dill: (Anethum graveolens) (A), Can be sown directly in garden after danger of frost is past. Likes humus and nutrient rich growing medium. Used in cooking and canning. Average ht. 30."

Fennel: (Foeniculum vulgare) (A), Prefers acidic soil. Used in the kitchen and for cosmetics. Average ht. 30."

Feverfew: (Chrysanthemum Parthenium) (P), may not survive as a perennial in cold, wet soil types or if allowed to go to seed. Used in floral arrangements, as an insect repellent, in cosmetics and potpourri.

Garlic: (Allium Sativum) (P), plant bulbs in spring. Harvest in fall. Best to replant bulbs in spring. Requires rich growing medium. Used for cooking, cosmetic, insect repellent and medicinal. Average ht. 24."

Horehound: (Marrubium vulgare) (P), does better in warmer climates in the North and/or good south facing sloped location. Used for a garden edging, bouquets, candy and coughdrops.

Hyssop: (Hyssopus officinalis) (P), well limed soil, will tolerate shade. Used for potpourri, white fly deterrent and cosmetics.

Lady's mantle: (Alchemilla vulgaris) (P), used for pillows for sleeping, floral arrangements, medicinal and cosmetic. Average ht. 12."

Lavender: (Lavendula angustifolia) (P), fairly easy to grow in most soil types. Used for potpourri, cosmetics, arrangements, and medicinal. Average ht. 24."

Lemon Balm: (Melissa officinalis) (P), grows in good to moderate soil. Full sun or partial shade. Used for cooking, potpourri and cosmetics. Average ht. 24."

Lemon Verbena: (Aloysia triphylla) (TP), requires rich growing medium. Used for cooking, potpourri, medicinal and cosmetic purposes. Average ht. 36."

Lovage: (Levisticum officinale) (P), requires rich, moist soil. Very good selection for North. Will grow in partial shade. Used as a substitute for celery in the kitchen. Also used as a salt substitute and for cosmetics. Average ht. 6'.

Mints: (Mertha family) (P), moist soil and partial shade to full sun. Used in cooking, potpourri, bouquets, medicinal and cosmetics. Mints are invasive and shouldn't be planted where they can choke out other plants. Average ht. 18-30".

Oregano: (Oreganum vulgare) (P), grows in good to moderate soil types. Used for cooking only. Average ht. 24".

Parsley: (Petroselinum crispum) (BI), requires rich soil, full sun or partial shade. Used to garnish dishes, nutritious when fresh. Also used in cosmetics. Attractive in flower gardens. Average ht. 12".

Pennyroyal: (Mentha pulegium) (P), moist soil, full sun or partial shade. Used as an insect repellent, potpourri and cosmetics. Average ht. 12".

Rosemary: (Rosmarinus officinalis) (TP), requires good to moderately rich soil types. Used for cooking, potpourri, cosmetics and incense. Average ht. 1-4".

Rue: (Ruta graveolens) (P), requires good to moderately rich soil type. Used as an insect deterrent, hedges and bouquets. Average ht. 24".

Sage: (Salvia officinalis) (P), requires well-limed soil. Used for cooking, cosmetics and medicinal. Average ht. 24".

Santolina: (Santolina chamaecyparissus) (P), requires good to average soil types. Good for hedges and potpourri. Average ht. 24".

Sorrel: (Rumex scutatus) (P), must be re-sown every third year. Requires good to average soil type. Used for cooking. Average ht. 18".

Southernwood: (Artemisia abrotanum) (P), requires good to average soil type. Uses include insect deterrent, potpourri, cosmetics, floral arrangements and wreaths. Average ht. 3'.

Summer Savory: (Satureja hortensus) (A), commonly referred to as the "green bean" herb. Used for cooking. Average ht. 18".

Sweet Woodruff: (Gallium odoratum) (P), requires all shade to partial shade in the North. Used for cooking, potpourri and ground cover. Average ht. 10".

Tansy: (Tanecetum vulgare) (P), toxic to cattle, avoid planting in or near pastures. Used for an ant and insect deterrent, fresh and dried floral arrangements, dye and cosmetics. Average ht. 3'.

Tarragon: (A. dracunculus) (P), requires good to average soil types. Used for cooking, cosmetics and for medicine. Average ht. 30".

Thyme: (T. vulgaris) (P), grows well in poor to average soil types. Used for cooking, cosmetics and medicinal.

Winter Savory: (Satureja montana) (P), hardy enough to survive our winters. Used for cooking. Average ht. 18."

REFERENCES

—*Rodale's Encyclopedia of Herbs,* Rodale Press, 1987.

—*The Pleasure of Herbs* by Phyllis Shaudys, Garden Way Publishing, 1986.

GROW HEALTHY, HARDY TREES AND SHRUBS

Someone asked me one time why I lived "all the way up there," referring to Michigan's Upper Peninsula.

I was actually stumped for a moment. It surely wasn't because of the long winters or the short growing seasons.

"There are more trees," I replied. It was a simple but honest answer. I love the endless miles of trees along the roadways. I love the trees that separate me from my neighbors. I love the long walks through the woods, staring up at the magnificent hemlocks, white pine and birch trees.

Perhaps that's why I've peppered my property with trees. Growing trees is a garden experience in itself. It takes a little trial and error, reading the books and talking to professionals to become successful at growing trees.

And patience. When you first plant a tree you're sure you'll never live long enough to see it grow tall. You'd be surprised. Like your kids, before long you're looking up at them!

Tree Selection

Success with trees has as much to do with tree selection as it does with planting and maintenance. Here's where purchasing trees from a discount retail store or at a bargain "downstate" can get you into trouble. Many retailers purchase trees wherever they can get the best bargain. I'm not saying you can't have good luck and save money by purchasing trees from a retail store. You can. However, you should be knowledgeable about what you're purchasing—its suitability to the region—before you open your wallet.

For instance, I wouldn't waste my money purchasing a weeping willow or a peach tree and expect to have success with it this far north (although you **will** find them sold this far north). Nor would I buy just any ol' type of apple or pear tree. The list of fruit trees at the end of this chapter will help you select varieties with proven track records in the northern regions.

You'll save money in the long run—and learn more about growing trees—if you purchase them from a local nursery or landscaping company. You may spend more money but it usually comes with planting advice and a guarantee of success. After you've spent all that time preparing a site and planting a tree you'll be glad you spent a few extra bucks for good plant stock.

Another way to ensure that a tree is hardy for the region is to transplant a native tree. Trees growing in our harsh weather climate will have a much better chance of survival than one grown in a nursery in Tennessee. Always obtain permission before you dig up a tree from private property. It's illegal to remove a tree from state or federal property.

Plant Hardiness

One thing we need to know about a tree is its degree of hardiness. If a tree is rated as hardy to -25 degrees (F) it means it will probably survive as long as the temperature doesn't drop below -25 (F). This is not always indicated on a tree purchased at a retail store or supermarket. However, folks at your local nursery should know a tree's hardiness rating. In addition, nursery catalogs, like Miller's and Gurney's, will also indicate a plant's degree of hardiness.

Hardiness is only part of the equation, however. There are other factors—some of which are beyond our control—which affect winter hardiness, such as weather and plant vigor.

For example, an exceptionally wet summer and fall can cause a tree to continue growing late into the season when it should be hardening off. Also, sudden changes of temperature during the winter, from very warm to cold, can also damage trees. These things are beyond our control. What we can control is how we take care of our trees from early spring until late fall. Careful pruning, fertilizing

(in the spring) and mulching all play a part in how "hardy" our trees will be when old man winter rears its ugly head.

According to Michigan State University horticulturist Steve Gregory, winter hardiness also depends on how well our plants grow during the season. Unfortunately, according to Gregory, trees and other plants which experience some type of stress during our short growing seasons will have a hard time rebounding before winter.

Remember, most tree growth takes place in the spring through early summer. That's when you need to fertilize. Late growth in the fall will delay a tree's natural inclination to harden off for the dormant winter months. In other words, lack of hardiness may get the blame for a tree's failure when in reality the tree didn't properly harden off for the winter.

Site Selection and Preparation

There are a number of things to consider when choosing a location for a tree. One of the biggest mistakes people make, I believe (because I've made it myself), is planting with the idea that the tree will "never get that big." It's hard to imagine a 8" pine seedling growing to a height of over 30 feet tall with an eight foot spread at its base.

People with limited space are often tempted to crowd trees. This will only result in slow growth and encourage insect infestation. Proper spacing can be determined by examining planting charts and talking to nursery folks. For instance, Christmas trees need to be about five or six feet apart. In contrast, blue spruce used for a windbreak, can be spaced up to ten feet apart. Also, consider the proximity to buildings, septic systems, propane tanks and power and phone lines. It can be expensive and a little disappointing later on to have to remove a beautiful tree to allow access to a septic tank in need of a cleaning!

Some trees need protection from the wind initially. For instance, my apple, pear, mountain ash and birch trees grow well in an area that is well protected from the wind (they're shielded by the tall spruce trees behind them). Newly planted

trees that are fairly large are the most susceptible to damage from the wind and may need staking.

It's surprising how well trees thrive in the different soil types in this region. Most trees don't require a specific soil type or pH level, although evergreens do better in a slightly acidic soil.

In summary, when selecting a site to plant a tree consider its proximity to structures, other trees and shrubs, soil type, drainage and need for wind protection.

Planting

After you've selected a site it's time to dig a hole for the tree you've just acquired. A good rule of thumb for hole size is to dig as deep as the root system is long (from the base of the tree) and twice as wide. Loosen up the sides of the trench with a spade or hoe; this will allow the spreading roots to penetrate into the surrounding soil.

Many soil types in the Midwest and Northeast are predominantly clay. Clay, of course, retains water longer in the spring, thus it takes longer for the soil to warm up. This can slow the growth of trees which need the warmth around the roots in the early spring to get started. One way to remedy this problem is to plant the balled plant with its roots halfway above grade. Good top soil is then added and tapered away from the base of the tree to create a berm. This berm will allow water to run off in the spring and allow warmth to penetrate into the roots of the trees.

Plant your trees immediately after you've purchased them, if possible. Choose and prepare your site ahead of time so you can set the plants in the ground as soon as you arrive home. Unfortunately, our busy lives don't allow for such an ideal situation. If you can't plant the trees right away keep the roots moist and protected from the wind and sun. I either wrap the balled root system in newspaper and soak with the garden hose or stick the bare roots into a bucket of water.

Trees purchased from a nursery or retail store come balled and burlap (B & B), root bound in large plastic containers, or sometimes as bare roots (large quantities of trees, such as Douglas Fir for Christmas trees or evergreens for wind-

breaks, are usually purchased as bare root stock). Remove all containers and wrappings from the bunched root systems, including the biodegradable ones. Tree roots purchased B & B are usually bunched up and need to be gently shaken loose so they have a chance to stretch out in the hole.

Don't hesitate to snip any roots that appear damaged or exceedingly long. Check for roots that are circling or girdling the root system. Girdling roots need to be removed. These are found wrapped around the trunk. They will hinder water intake and eventually strangle the plant.

Bare root stock should be visually inspected for damage to roots and possible girdling. Remove any packing material. Finally, trees should be soaked in water for a couple of hours before planting.

Follow the same planting procedures for balled and burlap stock as you would for bare root stock. Be sure all wrapping material is removed and inspect the roots for damage.

If you're transplanting a tree you've obtained from a neighbor, the procedure is a bit more time consuming. First, of course, you'll need to dig up the tree you intend to transplant. Larger trees require that you dig down into the root system, effectively severing the roots at a certain length. Transplants should be transported in water soaked wrappings of newspaper or placed in a bucket of water. Avoid exposure to

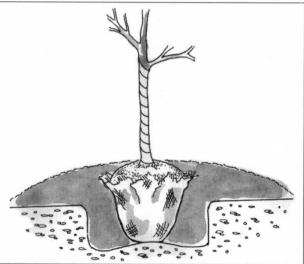

A good·way to plant trees and shrubs in heavy, wet soil is by forming an above ground berm for the root ball. With this method the root ball is set about 9-10 inches above grade (depending on the size of the root ball). Light soil is then tapered away from the top of the root ball. This will cause water to run off and the root ball will warm up quicker in the spring.

the wind and sun. Once they've arrived home you can treat them like bare root stock by soaking them overnight before planting.

Spread the roots around the hole as you backfill with soil. Contrary to popular belief, you should not backfill with amended soil. In other words, refill the hole you've dug with the same soil you've dug out of the hole. Studies have shown that backfilling entirely with peat or amended soil will cause excessive, unnatural growth of the root system.

Now pack the soil firmly into the hole, leaving a slight indentation to allow water to collect (unless drainage is a problem, then mound the soil around the trunk of the tree or use the berm method). And lastly, flood the area generously with your garden hose to flush remaining air pockets. Air pockets can kill new trees and shrubs.

Care and Maintenance

One of my favorite pastimes is to saunter around the yard and observe the progress of my various plants. I use this time to visually inspect my trees for any problems such as broken or weak limbs, insect infestation or damage to tree trunks. If I observe dead or dying limbs I can simply prune them away with my pruning shears. Insects can be collected for later identification; take note of what type of damage the insect may have caused. My local extension agent or nursery owner can usually tell me what to do about the critters. In other words, I don't have the time to study all the insects that attack trees—I just want to enjoy my trees and other plant life in the yard!

You may observe other things when you do your routine inspections. You may notice that a small tree needs support or marking so the neighbor kid doesn't mow over your seedling when you're away on vacation. You may even notice that a tree has died. If this is the case you should remove it and get ready to plant something in its place.

Actually, once trees are fully established they're fairly maintenance free (except for fruit trees). Annual pruning and regular inspections will reduce the amount of time spent fussing over your trees.

Fertilizing

All trees and shrubs require fertilizer to get off to a good start. A handful of an all purpose (10-10-10) inorganic fertilizer can be sprinkled around the base of your trees and shrubs in the early spring and summer only. There are also some organic products on the market which will offer slow, steady feeding of trees and shrubs such as Natural Guard fertilizer and Fertilome's Fish Emulsion. An application of Fertilome Winterizer fertilizer applied in September will improve winter hardiness. Otherwise, avoid fertilizing in the fall. Vigorous growth in the fall can be detrimental to a plant which should be starting to harden off.

For the organic gardener, there are organic methods to supply the essential nutrients (nitrogen, phosphorus and potassium) to trees and shrubs. The barrel that I fill 1/3 full with sheep manure catches rain from the eaves of my barn. I water my vegetables and trees with this solution. The content of this mixture contains a smaller percentage of the essential nutrients than does a commercial fertilizer. However, it is a good alternative for folks who wish to stay clear of inorganic fertilizers. There are organic fertilizers on the market such as Fruit Trees Alive!, offered by a company called Gardens Alive!

Mulching

The way you mulch your trees will have a lot to do with your personal preference and budget. All mulches achieve the same objective: to hold back the weeds, retain moisture, supply nutrients, and help protect the root systems from our harsh winters. Some mulches also provide a slow release of nutrients to the plant.

Sawdust. Sawdust is a good choice for a mulch; however, it robs nitrogen from the soil through the breakdown caused by microorganisms. Folks who live near a sawmill will want to take advantage of this inexpensive mulch. Just be sure to add a little nitrogen or an all purpose fertilizer to make up for the loss of nitrogen. A two inch layer of sawdust will provide good weed control around trees and shrubs.

Bark. Tree bark from redwood and other trees provides by far the most attractive, and relatively inexpensive form of mulch. This mulch is attractive when

used to landscape around businesses and modern homes. Shop around to find the best deal on tree bark.

Hay or straw. This is another good choice for a mulch, where available. Rural folks obviously have an inside track on this one. It may not be as attractive as bark but it's inexpensive and retains moisture extremely well. A 2-3 inch layer of hay or straw is all that's needed to benefit your fledgling trees. However, hay does contain a lot of weed seeds, which may be objectionable to some folks.

Manure. I swear by sheep manure not only for its water retention capabilities but for what I believe is a slow release of nutrients around the base of the plant. I use sheep and rabbit manure around my trees that I've got planted away from the house (for obvious reasons!).

Pine needles. Pine needles benefit acid-loving plants, thus it's a good choice for most trees and shrubs. A 2-3 inch layer will stave off the weeds.

Leaves. Tree leaves are an excellent choice for a mulch. Of course, they need to compact so they won't blow away. A 2-3 inch layer will help retain moisture and protect your plants over the winter.

Stones and rocks. A layer of white or colored stone is attractive around trees and ornamental shrubs. However, they don't trap moisture particularly well and tend to settle into the ground, making it a hassle to pick them out of the soil should you decide to get rid of them. Stones are better used for lining foot paths.

Watering

Rarely in the past few years has lack of water been a problem where I live in Michigan's Eastern Upper Peninsula. Quite the contrary. In my vegetable garden, I've had to keep the soil worked just to prevent that green scum from forming.

However, as sure as the snow flies in October there will be some dry summers, perhaps even droughts in the years ahead. These dry periods can be critical to trees and shrubs, particularly first and second year plants. That's why it's important to get trees and shrubs in early, to take advantage of April and May showers.

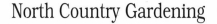
Late summer droughts will cause some shrubs, such as rhododendrons, to wilt. A good soaking with a garden hose will revive a drought-stressed shrub or tree. Inspect them in late summer, especially the first and second year plants. A good soaking with a hose and a fresh layer of mulch will aid in keeping these plants healthy and ready to sustain themselves through the winter months. However, remember never to apply fertilizer in late summer which will cause a spurt of growth when the plant should be getting ready to harden off.

Cold Climate Problems

In the North Country, snow is our natural ally for protecting plants. Regardless of how cold our winters are, a deep blanket of snow will usually protect plants from severe winter temperatures. We encounter problems when trees and other plants are planted, for instance, near driveways or windblown areas where the snow doesn't accumulate. Thus, it's important, in the planning stages, to avoid planting in these areas. Another way we can protect our cherished plants during the winter months is to apply a three to six inch base of straw, compost or well rotted manure around the base of our trees. Watch for rodents. While I've never noticed rodents burrowing into the mulch around my trees, it could be a problem. One safeguard against rodents is to leave a little open space near the trunk of the tree (you can also wrap the trunk with a commercial tree wrap which will protect against the rodents and severe cold).

As mentioned above, plants need to be suitable for our region to survive the cold winters. A plant can never assume hardiness qualities. Many trees are lost simply because they were never intended to survive in these parts. That is why it's best to purchase native stock from local nurseries.

Another way trees fall victim to the elements is due to rapid changes in weather. Unseasonably warm weather, followed by a sudden dip in the mercury, can kill them. Also, the absence of snow in late winter can weaken trees and cause root damage.

Winter kill is most noticeable in the spring. Some trees and shrubs will actually flower but then die. Unfortunately, little can be done to protect trees from win-

ter kill, with the exception of selecting stock hardy enough for the area and following a good plan of mulching, watering and fertilizing.

Winterburn is a winter malady common in the snow country. Evergreens that appear brownish, especially toward the top, are victims of winterburn. Winterburn occurs when the warmth of the winter sun dries out the needles, followed by bitterly cold winds.

Winterburn can be prevented by protecting the plants from the wind, shading them from the sun or covering them with a blanket. Smaller trees can also be protected by a blanket of snow, which, of course should be applied gently to avoid breaking any limbs. Prune away the dead foliage caused from winterburn, if the damage is not extensive. New growth will replace the damaged section of the tree or shrub.

Some broad-leaf evergreens, such as rhododendron, azalea, daphne and holly are particularly susceptible to winter injury. These shrubs are better off planted on the north, northeastern or east side of a home or building where they will be protected from the warm rays of the sun. Most ornamental shrubs need some type of wind protection, especially during the winter when the mercury dips down below zero, accompanied by those fierce northwest winds.

Tree trunks can also be damaged by fluctuations in temperatures. Red Maple and other smooth barked young trees are particularly susceptible to damage from the wind and cold. Young trees should always be wrapped with a commercial tree wrap. A tree wrap will also protect against animals and rodents that feed on the bark. Trunks can also be painted with an outdoor white latex paint to minimize injury from the elements.

Ice and snow are another potential problem in the winter. While snow protects trees and other plants, snow sliding off a roof on a warm sunny day can damage tree branches. Trees and shrubs can be protected by building wooden forts or tepees over the trees. The only disadvantage with this method of tree protection is the airflow inside the tepees doesn't provide the needed protection from the cold as does the snow. Tepees should be used on trees that could obviously be damaged by snow removal machinery or falling snow and ice.

PRUNING TOOLS

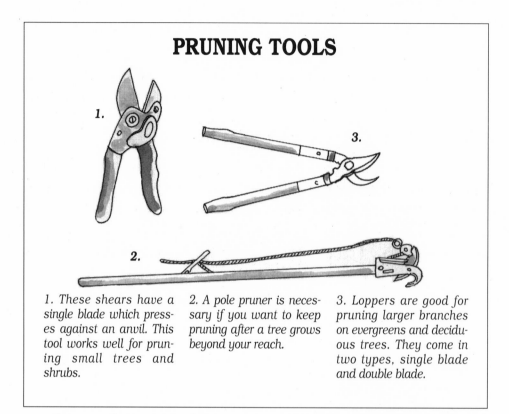

1. These shears have a single blade which presses against an anvil. This tool works well for pruning small trees and shrubs.

2. A pole pruner is necessary if you want to keep pruning after a tree grows beyond your reach.

3. Loppers are good for pruning larger branches on evergreens and deciduous trees. They come in two types, single blade and double blade.

Snow can become quite heavy on trees, especially on branches close to the ground. This can be avoided by regular pruning or tying them up prior to the onset of winter. You can also relieve snow laden limbs by dusting off the snow with a broom.

Likewise, falling ice can harm limbs. Wooden covers and tepees will provide protection from falling icicles. Another problem is ice buildup from freezing rain or an ice storm. Clinging ice on tree limbs is better left alone. As temperatures increase the ice will melt with minimal damage to the plants.

Pruning

The task of pruning trees is much like that of learning to ride a bicycle. We look forward to it with anxious anticipation. We want to learn a new skill but are afraid we'll fall flat on our face!

Fortunately, like bicycling, if we do make a mistake it's usually only a "skinned knee." This section is intended for those who wish to grow more healthy, compact trees for shade, beauty and fruit. Annual pruning will keep the job simple by avoiding the need for more complex pruning. You'll also save money by not having to hire a professional landscaper to take care of trees that have gotten out of hand.

By following a few easy steps and practicing on your trees, you'll gradually overcome your apprehension with pruning. In fact, there will come a day when you'll look forward to pruning much like you do other garden chores.

The objective of pruning any tree is to cut away dead or dying branches and to allow trees to assume their natural shape. Keep in mind that we can prune away a lot of limbs (within reason) without damaging a tree. Pruning is generally done during late winter or early spring before new growth occurs.

Newly acquired trees should be checked for broken or weak limbs prior to planting. Roots should also be examined, as mentioned previously, and pruned accordingly.

Deciduous Trees. Shade trees, like maples, oaks and poplars, should be pruned in late winter or early spring, before the sap flows. Young maples, beeches and birches can be pruned by simply clipping away the slender branches that have shot out past the others. This is called heading and involves making an angle cut just beyond a bud. Cutting on an angle allows water to run off the fresh cut.

Trimming is a cut that involves following a secondary branch back to where it originated on a primary branch. The branch or limb is then cut almost flush with the adjacent limb without leaving a stub, but rather a collar, which will appear after the cut has dried. These cuts should be reserved for the following purposes: to remove dead and dying branches, to remove a limb forming a narrow crotch, or to remove a limb that rubs or crosses another limb.

Evergreens. Folks who live in the country, like myself, probably don't care if their spruce and pine trees ever get pruned. In fact, I'd rather my spruce and pine trees, which provide excellent wind protection from the bitter northwest wind

don't get pruned. However, the spruce trees growing close to the house are another story. I would like to see these trees remain fairly small and compact—and attractive.

Pruning evergreens—or any trees—is all about deciding what you want from a tree. The trees growing close to my house are headed back each year by cutting away the "candle" that have outdistanced the others. This is usually done in early spring in the northern states. Never cut back the main leader unless you're removing a multiple leader. Dead and dying branches can be

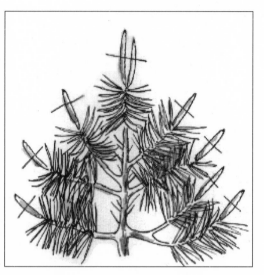

The candles, or new growth on evergreens, need to be trimmed back in early summer to encourage dense growth and a uniform shape for Christmas or ornamental trees.

trimmed back as can branches that are crossing or rubbing. This will allow light and air to penetrate the tree's interior.

Shrubs. Shrubs require regular pruning to avoid getting out of hand and becoming unsightly. Most of the major pruning of shrubs should be done in early spring, however they can be continued to be shaped throughout the summer, as needed.

You'll need a good set of hedge trimmers and pruning shears for the task. Your local extension agent and various books on shrubs and ornamentals will serve as excellent sources of pruning information. You may also want to hire a professional pruner or landscaper. By watching someone actually perform the task you can learn to do it yourself.

The main objective with shrubs is shaping them to your liking. It's kind of like giving your plant a haircut—only shrubs will stay still when you do it! And like getting a crew cut at the barber's, if it gets messed up, it will always grow back (within reason).

Christmas Trees

Many folks in the North see an opportunity in growing Christmas trees for fun and profit. Soil types in the northern regions are primarily acidic which is ideal for growing Douglas Fir, Blue Spruce and Scotch Pine, all good choices for Christmas trees.

The marketability of Christmas trees for the small tree farmer depends a lot on supply and demand. Folks living near heavily populated areas may have difficulty competing with commercial growers who offer trees at a discount in front of retail stores. Those living in sparsely populated areas may have better luck making a profit from Christmas trees due to the customer's distance from the city.

White pine are fast growing trees which can be used for windbreaks and Christmas trees.

Christmas trees grown for the holiday season take about eight to ten years to reach their desired height. Fertilizing, mulching and regular pruning are very important for a well managed Christmas tree lot. Douglas fir, scotch pine, white pine, and blue spruce are the most popular evergreens used for decorating during the holidays.

Windbreaks

There is a wind that blows across an open field to the west of our home which comes straight down from Canada (they must have a big fan up there they turn on in the winter!). I've managed to buffer this breeze with a solid row of pines and spruces I inherited when I bought this property. These trees were planted in a long single row. Windbreaks are more effective at holding back those "Alberta Clippers," as one local radio personality calls them, if planted two or three rows deep.

North Country Gardening

by Neil Moran

This row of trees forms a windbreak to protect the author's home from those nasty nor'westers.

Most evergreens make good windbreaks, though the spruces are probably the best. However, spruce are slower growing than the pines, thus you'll have to wait longer for the spruces to be of any benefit. It's best then, to plant a variety of trees for a windbreak. This will also minimize problems with insects and diseases.

Hardy Fruit Trees

One spring, several years ago, I painstakingly planted over 20 fruit trees received as a gift. Not one of them survived. The trees were purchased in Michigan's Lower Peninsula, which may explain part of this failure. However, I can't deny the fact I made some mistakes which attributed to their demise.

Fruit trees can be grown successfully in the North. Apple, plum and sour cherries grow relatively well in this region. However, it's a little more difficult, but not impossible, to grow a peach or pear tree in the short season zones.

This section will save you a lot of trial and error, and money, by introducing you to the basics of fruit tree selection, location, planting, feeding and preparation for winter.

Choosing a Fruit Tree

So how can we ensure success growing fruit trees in this harsh climate? Careful selection of plant stock is the first step. This aspect of planting fruit trees cannot be taken lightly. Many a dollar will be wasted, not to mention time and effort, by purchasing trees that don't have a prayer in the harsh weather zones. Whether you order from a catalog or purchase from a reputable nursery, be sure the trees you buy can survive our harsh climate.

The best bet appears to be to buy fruit trees that have been grafted from native trees. For instance, Yellow Transparents, an especially hardy apple tree for zones three and four, is best suited for this climate if grafted with a native species that has performed well in this country.

Although pear, apple and plum trees grow in this area, not all cultivars can take our harsh winters. You have to become familiar with particular varieties suitable to our hardiness zones. For example, Gurney's Nursery out of Yankton South Dakota, sells a Haralson and a Fireside apple that I've recently acquired for my yard. These apples are listed as hardy in zones 3-8. In contrast, Granny Smith and McIntosh simply won't make it in the North. When choosing fruit trees, be sure you purchase at least two different varieties to insure proper pollination.

One final note on fruit tree selection: stay away from dwarf fruit trees. The hardiness of current rootstocks is questionable. And remember, a poor cultivar will always be poor regardless of the culture it receives.

Planting and Location

Fruit trees grow well in a slightly acidic soil. A well drained sandy loam soil is best for fruit trees due to its water and nutrient retention capability. Avoid planting in heavy clay which doesn't provide adequate drainage. You can improve a slightly heavy or sandy soil by adding compost or well rotted manure prior to planting.

North Country Gardening
by Neil Moran

One of the biggest problems with growing fruit trees in the northern region, besides finding hardy plant stock, is the heavy, damaging snows. Avoid planting near buildings and under other trees where snow may drift, causing limb breakage.

Should fruit trees be planted in the fall or spring? If your summers are hot and dry and winters mild, plant in the fall. If winter comes early and the temperature frequently dips below zero, plant in the spring. This will give the trees time to establish themselves before the snow flies. I think it's safe to say most northern gardeners (except those living in a warmer micro climate) should plan on planting fruit trees in the spring, especially if planting bareroot stock. Potted trees can be planted a little later in the spring or early summer.

Preparing a site is the next step. Dig a hole that is deep enough to set trees fairly deep—and more importantly—wide enough to allow roots to spread easily in their new location. Suggested width is twice the length of the root system. A spade usually leaves the side of a hole smooth or shaved, so rough the sides up with a garden fork or spade; this will make it easier for the roots to expand.

After you've set your tree into the hole, cover and pack firmly with top soil. To avoid air pockets, flood the area around the base of the tree with copious amounts of water from a garden hose.

Folks dealing with clay can plant fruit trees using the same method I've mentioned for other trees. Be sure to amend the soil with a good top soil and stake the tree if necessary. And remember to plant fruit trees with the graft union about two inches above the soil level or grade.

Fruit trees will do better if allowed wind protection and/or a south facing slope. Never crowd fruit trees in with other trees. Fruit trees need ample sunlight to set fruit each year, especially here in the North. Also, avoid planting where the young tree will get trampled by animals or children playing.

Feeding, Pruning and Mulching

Fruit trees need to get off to a good start in the spring. That's when most of your fertilizing will take place. A soil test will help you determine what your trees

will need. Manure tea or a commercial fertilizer such as Miracle Grow or Rapid Grow is recommended. Fertilizer stakes can be purchased from nurseries and are also a good choice for feeding hungry trees.

Never fertilize towards the end of summer or early fall, especially with nitrogen. Late fall growth is not good for fruit trees. Winter kill is more likely on a fruit tree that is growing vigorously in the fall, instead of preparing to go dormant as it should.

I mulch all my trees in the fall and have been amazed at the steady growth I've seen in not only my fruit trees, but my Red Maple, Mountain Ash and evergreens. Different mulches can be used such as grass clippings, sphagnum peat moss and old straw. I use sheep manure mixed half and half with old hay. I believe this mixture smothers the weeds and retains moisture while providing nutrients (the following year) to the young trees. In addition, a 6-8 inch cover of mulch will provide considerable protection against the severe winter weather.

Pruning

According to Steve Gregory, the MSU tree specialist, the only difference between pruning fruit trees in the North and pruning in the South is we need to do it more often in the North. Perhaps this has a lot to do with the rain we get in the area and suitable growing conditions for most trees.

A once-per-year pruning is ideal. Pruning really doesn't take a lot of time and it provides me with a lot of enjoyment as I walk around my yard inspecting my trees, in addition to the flowers and birds at the feeder.

Why prune fruit trees? Pruning fruit trees is done for several reasons:

1. To cut away foliage and allow the sun access to the tree (especially important in this region).

2. To allow fewer, but larger fruit to develop and ease the burden on the tree of producing a lot of fruit.

3. To cut away dead or dying branches that will suck the energy out of the tree.

HARDY FRUIT TREES

PLUMS
Zone 3
Tecumseh
Pembina
Underwood
LaCrescent
Waneta
Zone 4
Superman
Mt. Royal
Alderman
Zone 5
Pipestone
Toka

APPLES
Zone 4
Cortland
Yellow Transparent
Chestnut Crab
Honey Gold
Jonathon
Haralson*
Redwell
Zone 3
Sweet sixteen
Red Baron
Red Dutchess
Mantet
Hazen

CRABAPPLE
Dolgo*
Chestnut
Centennial
*suggested for beginners

CHERRY
Montmorency
Nanking cherry
North star**
Nanking cherry**

SANDCHERRY-PLUM HYBRIDS
Red diamond**
Sapalta
Compass

HARDY APRICOTS
Harcot
Hargrand
Moongold**
Sungold**

PEARS
Parker**
Luscious**
Gourmet
Summer Crisp

**May not be suitable in zone 3 and areas of the North where winters are particularly severe.

KIWI
"Arctic Beauty" Kiwi, includes the following Russian varieties which are hardy to Zone 3 or -40°F
(these are offered by Northwoods Nursery: see *Sources for Seeds and Equipment*).

Krupnopladnaya
Pavlovskaya
Urozainaya
Nahodka
Sentyabraskaya

SHRUBS FOR THE NORTH

Shrubs should be a part of your overall landscape design. Use them to create borders, foot paths and to hide unsightly areas in a yard. Shrubs can also be planted to attract honey bees and birds to the yard.

If planted in the right location and cared for properly, some exotic species of shrubs will do well in the North. PJM rhododendron, saucer magnolias and lace leafed Japanese maple have all been grown successfully in the cold climates. However, be sure they're protected from the wind and cared for by pruning, feeding and mulching.

It looks like these lilacs outlived the occupants of this country farm house.

These potentilla shrubs thrive in this rock garden near the Valley Camp museum in Sault Ste. Marie, Michigan.

Shrubs can be planted above grade in clay areas by creating a berm as suggested for trees.

SURE BET SHRUBS FOR THE NORTH

Barberry
Buffaloberry
Dwarf burning bush
Dwarf mugho pine
Ginnala maples
Honeysuckle
Juniper
Lilac (including Korean, purple Persian, old fashioned)
Meadowlark forsythia
Mock orange
Mountain laurel
Roses (old fashioned and hybrid teas)
Siberian pea shrub
Spirea
Yew

Roses

Roses like a slightly acidic soil and can tolerate a little clay if amended with organic matter such as sphagnum peat moss, well rotted barn manure and grass clippings.

Folks in the know about roses highly recommend the purchase of roses from garden catalogs or local nurseries. They don't trust the quality of a rose bought in a supermarket. Here again, as with fruit trees and other plants, a couple extra dollars spent on quality roses will be beneficial in the long run. What we should be trying to do in our yards and gardens is create a lasting landscape, one that will not only survive the harsh winters, but thrive to produce a beautiful bounty of color and fruit.

Hybrid tea roses grow well in the North if properly maintained.

169

North Country Gardening

by Neil Moran

Location and Soil Preparation

Roses require at least five hours of sun each day. Morning sun is preferred to dry off the morning dew. Well drained soil is a must. A rich loamy soil is preferred but as mentioned, clay and sand soil types can be amended with organic material. Dig a hole about two feet deep and fill it with two or three shovels full of well rotted manure or compost prior to planting.

The only time to plant roses in the North is in the spring. Rose beds should be prepared the summer before planting, if possible. For new sites the sod needs to be completely removed and the ground worked thoroughly to eliminate trouble-some weeds and rhizomes. Try to avoid planting near trees where the roots will interfere with your roses.

Rose Selection and Planting

Selecting the right roses is like choosing the right candy in a candy store. You're enticed by all the different colors and "flavors" to choose from. The hybrid tea varieties perform the best in northern areas, although many folks have luck with grandifloras and floribundas as well.

If you're ordering roses through the mail it's a good idea to let the nursery folks know when you want them delivered to your home. In other words, don't depend on them to choose the time they think is best to send them. They will invariably send them too soon. For some reason the word just hasn't gotten out how late spring is in coming in the North Country!

Roses should arrive when all frost is out of the ground and snow has left the woods. The soil doesn't necessarily have to be warm yet. Plant right away, if possible. Roses generally come bare root as opposed to potted. Check the roots for any broken or dangling roots. Prune if necessary.

Roses should be spaced a minimum of 24 inches apart. Shrub roses, such as Golden Wings and Blanc Double de Coubert, should be spaced according to potential size, up to six feet apart.

Dig a hole 15 inches deep and leave a cone of soil in the center to drape the roots over so they spread in all directions. In colder climates such as ours, the bud

union should be 1-2 inches below the surface of the soil. The bud union is a swollen point where a rose has been grafted and is used to gauge planting depth.

Feed roses, initially, with superphosphate worked into the soil at planting time. This will encourage early root growth. Don't expect having cut roses to show off to your neighbors the first year. However, this is possible providing we have a relatively warm summer. I've observed first year hybrid teas blossom quite well even during a cooler-than-usual summer.

The canes of bare root roses need some protection from the wind and sun until the roots are well established. Take a garden spade and mound soil around and over top of the canes. A couple of weeks later, begin to remove the soil until all is removed over a ten day period.

Fertilizing and Mulching

Roses are hungry critters so you will need to have a complete fertilizer, such as 7-7-7 or 5-10-5 on hand. Single blooming roses need a spring and an early summer application of fertilizer. Repeat bloomers need at least three feedings: early spring and after each period of blooming. Never fertilize in the fall when the plant is hardening off for the winter.

Roses need rain—at least an inch a week. If it doesn't rain, they rely on you to get out the hose and soak it to them. To avoid diseases caused by mildew, water should be applied directly to the soil as opposed to the plant.

Mulch to keep the ground moist and ward off the weeds. Compost, grass clippings, ground bark and pine needles all work well. Mulches will need to be pushed away to allow for fertilizing.

Pests and Diseases

We're fortunate here in the North we don't have the insect problems our southern neighbors do (we have enough problems when it comes to gardening!). However, we need to be on the look out for aphids, spider mites, leafhoppers and thrips. These creatures can be easily controlled with applications of insecticidal soaps, rotenone or pyrethrum.

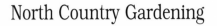

Due to our more-often-then-not damp weather, we need to be concerned about a few diseases that afflict roses; namely, powdery mildew, blackspot and rust. These can be avoided by spacing plants properly, allowing air circulation and avoiding planting under tree branches and rain gutters.

Care and Maintenance

Roses do require a fair amount of attention. The reason we garden is because we enjoy fussing with our plants. If we learn the basics of caring for roses it will become an enjoyable learning experience.

Roses can withstand our winters, believe it or not. But they need protection. One method to protect the canes from the elements is to cover the entire cane with hay and soil. This is done when the weather is cool but before the ground freezes. Be generous and mound the plant with a thick layer of soil and organic material.

Another more costly but perhaps more effective way to protect roses over winter, is to purchase the styrofoam cones. These cones slip right over the rose bush and can be left on until things thaw out in the spring.

Roses need annual pruning. This is done in the spring, the same time that the soil and/or mulch is removed from around the plant. Hybrid teas and floribundas should be pruned back to 12 to 15 inches. Grandifloras can be pruned to 18-24 inches. Pruning is done much like trees, that is, a 45 degree cut beyond a bud needs to be done with a sharp pair of pruners. Avoid ragged cuts that encourage disease.

Shrub roses and English roses need only a slight pruning to shape the plant.

LAWNS

I've concluded, via casual observation about the North Country, that folks "up here" aren't real fussy about their lawns. It's not that our lawns are shabby. In fact, they're usually quite lush even in August when the lawns in the rest of the country are drying up due to the heat and dry spells.

Perhaps it's the fact that we savor our short summer so much that we don't want to spend too much of it fussing over grass. Or maybe it's just that "laid back" spirit in the North: we don't need to keep up with the Jones in this neck of the woods.

Whatever the reason, most of us desire some open space in our yards. Although most northerners love the woods, we also desire the open space of a lawn. Lawns aren't terribly difficult to establish in the North. And, once started, they tend to grow well with little maintenance.

What does plague lawns in this country, however, is the occasional brown spots in our yards due to ice build up or heavy snow which can encourage diseases. Moles also tend to be a problem. They love to burrow under the snow and right into the sod, leaving conspicuous holes in our yards. Finally, weeds travel from afar, land and flourish in our yards due to the wet, cool climate that encourages germination. We can either "stop and smell the dandelions" or seek and destroy these "intruders" with toxic chemicals. I take a live and let live approach to my yard.

Preferred Soil Type

You need good soil to grow an attractive, low maintenance lawn cover. Unless it tests high in phosphorus, work in a phosphate fertilizer (such as 18-46-0) prior to planting. Apply 5 pounds of phosphate per 1000 square feet. If you've recently built a home and have a decision as to what type of top soil is brought in, by all means take a little time and insist your contractor deliver a good quality top soil.

There are no short cuts here. A good top soil should contain at least 75% good black dirt with the rest a sandy loam. A little clay mixed in is sometimes inevitable in this country but it won't stop you from growing a good lawn cover. A six to eight inch layer of top soil is sufficient to establish a good lawn cover.

If you're re-seeding an area you may want to bring in some well rotted compost or barn manure to amend the soil, especially if your soil is heavy or sandy. Work it into the soil with a roto-tiller. Or, you can simply purchase topsoil to improve the top layer of your lawn.

For newly landscaped areas have the contractor do the initial spreading of the soil with a bulldozer, then finish leveling and smoothing by hand with a garden rake; break up the dirt balls as best you can with a garden rake.

Seed Mixtures

The most common ingredient in a lawn seed mixture for the northern region is Kentucky Bluegrass. Common Kentucky Bluegrass is grown successfully from North Dakota to northern Maine. Bluegrass has a resilient underground rhizome system that once established, can take a lot of traffic. Lawn seed mixture, therefore, should be at least 50% bluegrass.

Park Kentucky Bluegrass, developed in Minnesota, is a preferred lawn seed. It establishes itself quicker than other types of bluegrass and tends to green up sooner in the spring.

Bluegrass is usually mixed with creeping red fescue which is more shade tolerant than bluegrass. Red fescue also establishes a strong rhizome system. Finally, a good seed mixture should contain a small percentage of perennial rye grass.

A good mix for the cold climate zones then, should include approximately 55-60% Kentucky bluegrass, 30% creeping red fescue and 10-15% perennial rye grass. Check the ingredients on a bag of lawn seed before opening your wallet. Be

wary of "bargains" which may contain an abundance of annual ryegrass and weed seeds. Annual ryegrass will give the initial appearance of a successful lawn cover, only to be replaced by weeds the following year.

Buying from a local nursery (or taking the time to carefully examine the ingredients on a bag of lawn seed) will ensure you have a mixture that will thrive here in the North. Once you get a lawn started, it really will thrive, unless of course, your soil type is extremely sandy or clay.

Planting a Lawn Cover

Now you're ready to plant. The best time to plant a lawn cover is in mid-May or late August, providing the soil is moist. Lawn seed can be planted either with a seed spreader or by hand. Figure on using three pounds for every 1000 square feet. There are no short cuts here either.

A water-filled "rolling pin" should be used to pack down your newly planted seed. Some folks also cover the seed with straw. If planting during a relatively dry period, this may be necessary, otherwise don't waste your time and money covering with straw. Simply spread the seed, pack it and in a few short weeks you'll be rolling in the grass!

North Country Gardening

by Neil Moran

REFERENCES

—*Rodale's Illustrated Encyclopedia of Gardening and Landscaping Techniques* (Chemical Free), Barbara W. Ellis, Editor, Rodale Press Emmaus, Pennsylvania.

—*Planting and Care of Ornamental Landscape Plants*, Michigan State University, Cooperative Extension Service.

—*The Northern New England Master Gardener Reference Manual*, Volume 2, 2nd Edition, 1994 University of Maine Cooperative Extension.

—*Rodale's Illustrated Encyclopedia of Gardening and Landscaping Techniques*, Rodale Press, Inc. 1990 Barbara W. Ellis, Editor.

—*Cold Climate Gardening*, by Lewis Hill, Garden Way Publishing, 1987.

—*Step-by-Step Rose Growing for Beginners*, Doug Hall Flower & Garden Special Rose Issue, May 1994.

—*All About Roses, Ortho Books*, Project Editor, Susan Lang, Writers Rex Wolfe, James McNair.

—*A Beautiful Lawn Can Be Yours*, Ronald C. Smith and Dale E. Herman, North Dakota State University Extension Service, Fargo ND.

—*Tree Fruit Culture and Varieties in North Dakota*, Robert G. Askew, Larry Chaput and Ronald Smith, North Dakota State University Extension Service, Fargo ND.

—*Timbercrest's Easy Gardening Leaflet*, Ed. 28, Summer 1994, Marquette, Michigan.

—*Home Fruit Cultivars For Northern Wisconsin*, B.R. Smith & T.R. Roper, University of Wisconsin Extension, Madison Wisconsin.

BUILD A WATER GARDEN

Water cascades gently down a rocky falls. Tropical fish glisten as they rise to the surface of the water and kiss the sun. Meanwhile, hummingbirds and bumble-bees hum past on their way to their favorite flowers and shrubs. And there you sit, in the midst of this scene of serenity, relaxing from a hard day at work.

Most folks associate water gardens with golf courses, city parks or Busch Gardens. However, they're becoming increasingly popular among home gardeners, even here in the North. They're a great way to add a little sound, movement and aquatic life to our floral and shrub gardens.

According to Betsy Berry, owner of Circle B Landscape & Nursery in Gaylord, Michigan, water gardens are gaining popularity in the north. She said when people see their neighbor with one they've just got to have one of their own.

The water garden which has been in our front yard for a few years now is testimony to the fact water gardens will do well in the harsh weather climates. Also, that nowadays they're relatively inexpensive and easy to install. Our harsh winters and short seasons will, however, pose some unique problems for water gardens. These obstacles can be easily dealt with by following a few precautions, which I'll get to in a moment.

Choosing a Pond

The ponds for water gardens come in three types: concrete, prefabricated and the flexible liner. Sizes range from about 4 feet by 4 feet to 12 feet by 16 feet. The prefabricated and flexible liners cost between $80 to $300. The concrete gardens are much more expensive—around $2000—and must be installed with heavy equipment. You can build your own cement water garden; however, the best laid plans can result in a leaky pond.

North Country Gardening

by Neil Moran

You're only limited by your imagination when it comes to designing a water garden.

The plastic prefabricated water gardens and flexible liners offer the easiest and most practical solution to adding a water garden to your landscaping plans, according to Jay Pacaro, owner of Weber's Floral in Sault Ste. Marie, Michigan. They're light, easy to install, and will last for years without leaking.

Location

Consider the overall location of your water garden in relation to your house, deck, flower gardens and recreation areas. The pond my wife installed in our front yard is a plastic prefabricated pond. She surrounded her pond with perennials, annuals and small shrubs. The pond sits about ten feet in front of our deck. A petunia lined walkway leads from the deck to the pond. The deck, pond, flowers and trees blend in nicely to achieve the effect we were looking for.

A water garden must be within reach of a garden hose and electrical supply for a pump and other accessories you may wish to add, such as patio lights.

Locate away from trees, if possible, to avoid autumn leaves filling your pond. If you must install your pond under a tree consider purchasing a mesh type material, such as the type used to protect strawberries from birds, to catch the falling leaves. Nearby trees also make for some difficult digging when installing a liner.

Adding Rocks and a Pump

Here is where my wife used her imagination to create the effect she desired. And you can too. You'll need a couple of wash tubs full of rocks to create a waterfall and to line the outside rim of your pond. Actually, in the process of landscaping around your pond, you'll be constructing a rock garden as well. Choose rocks—such as limestone or sandstone—native to your area. Layered rock, such as sandstone, is preferable for stacking to create a waterfall effect. Native rock (most of the Upper Peninsula lies on top of Jacobsville Sandstone left by the glaciers) can be obtained cheaply or at no cost at all from a neighbor or friend. My wife cruised the side streets in town until she found someone who was willing to part with a pile of rocks. And of course, you can purchase rocks from a contractor or nursery.

Arrange the flat rock in a vertical fashion behind the pond (facing your house or wherever you want to view the pond from). The hose from the water pump can then be snaked up behind the pile of rocks and out of sight until it reaches the top where it can send water cascading down the "falls." This will add a very tranquil quality to your water garden. It also attracts hummingbirds, frogs, butterflies and other wildlife to the area.

Water pumps can be purchased at nurseries or by mail order for around $80. The pump should lie at the deepest end of the pond and be plugged-in, preferably, to a grounded outlet nearby. Seek the advice of a licensed electrician before you install an electric supply.

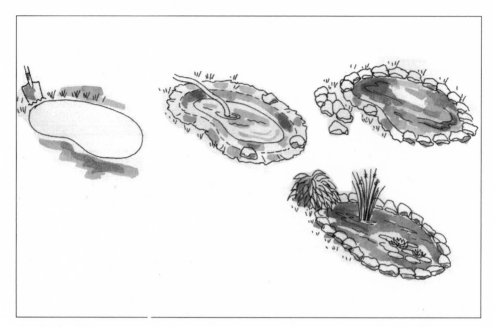

1. The first step to installing a plastic liner for a water garden is to outline the shape with a flexible water hose or rope. Next, remove the sod with a spade or garden fork and dig the hole to the depth required (refer to instructions that come with the liner).

2. Now lay the liner into the crater and hold in place with medium-size ' rocks. Fill the pond with water. Adjust the liner for a smooth fit as you fill the pond.

3. After it's filled with water, lay more stone around the edges and conceal with rocks or a ground cover.

4. Water lilies and bog plants can be planted right into the pond. You can also add goldfish and other attractive fish. Fish and plants keep your pond clean.

Installation of Prefabricated and Flexible Liners

One person can easily handle the task of installing a pond. However, you can do what my wife did. She invited a friend over to help her install the pond, which they did within a couple of hours.

Start by outlining the shape of the pond with flexible water hose or rope. Dig to the depth you need depending on the height of the pond you've purchased. Layer your hole with a little sand and dig out the bottom of the hole as evenly as possible so your pond will be level.

Level the rims of the pond. An uneven liner will look awkward, and should it overflow with water, it will dump its excess to one end of the pond, making that end quite soggy.

If installing a flexible liner, follow the instructions above. When finished, place heavy rocks along the entire edge of the liner material to hold it in place.

Now you're ready to fill the pond. You will need to be within reach of a garden hose to accomplish this task. The smallest prefab ponds and liners hold around 60 gallons. A 12 foot long, 6 foot wide and 16 inch deep pond will hold about 500 gallons of water. Incidentally, if done right, you'll only have to clean and refill the pond once a year.

Plants and Fish For the Water Garden

Plants and fish can be added to the water garden a little each season. Avoid the temptation to grow more plant life and fish than a pond can handle. What you're creating is an ecological balance between fish, plant life, insects and algae (this ecological balance is also what keeps your pond clean).

Less than half of your pond surface should be covered with plant life. This will allow you the opportunity to see fish swimming underneath. Limit your fish to no more than a dozen per 4 foot by 4 foot section of pond area.

Water lilies can be planted in the pond and are very attractive when in bloom. They need to be rooted in containers seated at the bottom of the pond. Lilies are rather expensive and need to be removed and placed in a cellar or inside a house over the winter, at least in the northern areas. Lilies are suitable for the larger water gardens or spring fed ponds.

Bog plants, also known as emergent and marginal plants, include some hardy types such as, pickerel weed, arrowheads, cattails and yellow water iris; shorter species include golden-club, parrot's feather and spike rush. Bog plants root beneath the water or in the shallow water at the edges of the pond and grow skyward, projecting their pretty blooms to the heavens.

Goldfish, golden orfe, and different types of fantail fish are surprisingly hardy for the northern pond, once established. Before you add fish, test city water for chlorine dioxide and chloramine. Both of these can be treated with chemicals purchased at a nursery or pet shop.

When you bring fish home from the pet shop or department store, allow them to adjust to the change in temperature of their new habitat. Place the bag and all into the pond and leave it a couple hours. The best time to do this is when the outside temperatures have warmed your pond. An aquarium thermometer will take the guess work out of this. The temperature of the water in your pond should be above 50 degrees at the time you plant your fish. You may lose a few fish at first, thus it's best not to invest too much in this aspect of your water garden project right away. Although fish will scavenge for insects and plant life in the pond you will need to feed them fish food daily. Avoid heavy feeding in the fall—fish don't digest food well in cool weather.

Bringing the Fish Inside

You'll have to remove the fish from your pond in the winter, unless your pond is very deep (over five or six feet). In the warmer climates fish stay in small ponds all winter. This isn't possible in this country where the ice in the pond may freeze right to the bottom! My wife brings her fish inside to an aquarium.

Used aquariums can be purchased for a fraction of the cost of a new one. A lot of people get into this hobby for a short time then eventually give it up. Look for used aquariums at garage sales and flea markets.

Fill your aquarium with cold water and ice to avoid the shock of a sudden change of temperature when the fish are removed from the pond (assuming this is being done late in the fall). Check the temperature before transferring your fish into the aquarium. It may take a day or so for the fish to adjust to the change before resuming normal swimming and feeding habits.

Landscaping with Plants and Flowers

Here again you can use your imagination to create the "look" you have in mind. In fact, you're only limited by your imagination—and money—when it comes to what you can plant around your pond. Ground hugging plants such as ground ivy and lady's mantle can be planted around the edge of the pond and between the rocks that line the pool to conceal the rim of the liner. Pansies, petunias, dahlias, begonias, lilies and even small shrubs can be planted so they extend a few feet to several feet away from the actual pond.

While you're at it, choose plants and shrubs, such as honeysuckle and barberry, which will attract birds and other wildlife to your water garden. In addition to bees, hummingbirds and song birds, we've had sharptail grouse visit our pond. And one day a visiting beagle couldn't resist the temptation and jumped right in!

You can expand your satisfaction with gardening by building a beautiful water garden, surrounded by your favorite perennials and annuals. It's a great way to relax at the end of a busy day—whether it be from cutting wood or working at the office.

REFERENCES

Build a Garden Pond, by Neil Moran, Michigan Country Lines, May/June 1994.
Garden Pools & Fountains, Ortho Books, Edward B. Claflin 1988.

MARKET GARDENING FOR FUN AND PROFIT

For retiree Amy Van Ooyen and her "Golden Girls," market gardening in Iron County in Michigan's Upper Peninsula is as much a social gathering as it is a business venture. These folks come together each Saturday during harvest time to share their produce—and stories—with each other and anyone who cares to stop by.

Of course, us northerners don't grow the volume or variety of produce for market like folks in the southern regions of the U.S. Likewise, you don't see the roadside stands in the North, stocked with cantaloupe, corn and juicy red tomatoes like you do down south.

However, you do see smaller fruit and vegetable stands with an ample offering of root crops: potatoes, carrots and onions. These veggies provide excellent ingredients for the Finnish pasties prepared by folks in Michigan's Upper Peninsula.

Occasionally, we northerners hit on a bounty year and can dress up our market stands with sweet corn, squash and pumpkins. We can also purchase produce from our southern neighbors to offer to our friends and regular customers.

Getting Started

You can start up a market gardening venture for a relatively small investment of time and money. An old pick-up truck or van with a good place to park—or a table with an umbrella over it in your front yard—will do. More sophisticated sellers like Charlie and Kathy Nye of Hessel, Michigan, operate a produce market out of their garage each summer. Their home market is complete with weighing scale, refrigerator and an attractive sign out front to encourage folks to stop and shop (or just say "hello").

You'll need to define your market. Will you sell wholesale or to retailers? You'll make more money selling wholesale than to a retailer; however, you'll have to do the actual selling. If you decide to sell large quantities to retailers, find out ahead of time what these folks are willing to pay for your produce. Compare this with other retailers. Try to have backup customers should one of your retailers discontinue purchasing your vegetables.

One especially good market for produce is restaurants which purchase fresh vegetables, particularly gourmet items. Popular restaurants in the area may be just the customers you're looking for, if you've got what they want.

Location is undoubtedly important. If you're not located on a well traveled road you should be near one or not far out of town. If you live in the country you may need to advertise, at least until word gets out that you're in business.

The demand for fresh vegetables is so great that the Nyes can't keep up with the orders from regular customers (which includes tourists and folks who spend their summers near Hessel). The Nyes live a couple miles on the outskirts of this harbor town of about 200 year-round residents. Even though these folks aren't located on the main thoroughfare to town, word has gotten out they sell quality organic vegetables at a reasonable price.

Market gardening is as popular as ever. Perhaps this is one business entity the large retailers can't take away from us! It makes sense. It's hard to compare fresh produce with the store bought kind trucked in from California. And truly fresh produce can only be acquired from folks who grow it locally. Thus, the home gardener who sells produce at a stand in their front yard or on a corner downtown can profit from this endeavor.

Selecting and Preparing Produce

Considerably more planning is needed to grow vegetables for market than for the home garden. It's critical, if your business is to succeed, to grow what people want and have it ready when they want it. Both of these objectives can be difficult to live up to, especially in the northern states where the growing conditions can be tentative at best.

North Country Gardening

Charlie and Kathy Nye sell organically-grown produce out of their garage in Hessel, Michigan.

It's good to have a staple crop that will survive some of the more disappointing growing seasons. Potatoes, carrots, peas, hybrid (early) sweet corn, beans and some of the cole crops are the best candidates. Even in the worst years you should get plenty of these vegetables to sell to your hungry customers. Folks who have experienced a few summers in the North will understand if your watermelon and tomatoes didn't ripen!

Practice succession planting so you can keep your stand stocked with a variety of offerings. However, folks who love fresh vegetables—and most folks do—will buy what you've got just to be able to eat fresh produce.

Preparing Vegetables for Display

Vegetables have to be appealing to the eye. A dirty carrot may be a carrot just the same, to some folks, but other folks won't go near it at a produce stand. They want fresh, bright and clean vegetables to take home. Thus you'll need to wash some of your produce, particularly the root crops.

Also, be sure there are no bugs on your vegetables. Personally, if I see a cabbage looper on a head of broccoli I'm fixing to eat I simply brush it off before I eat it. I may even wash the broccoli! Other folks think this is cause to throw the vegetable away. Don't take a chance of losing a customer and your good reputation. Be sure your market produce is free of critters.

Getting Noticed

Market gardeners who set up a roadside stand along the highway should have an attractive or otherwise noticeable sign to encourage passing motorists to stop. A roadside stand need not be flashy. However, it should be advertised well ahead of speeding cars. Thus, you'll need to place a sign advertising your business along the shoulder of the road at least 500 feet ahead of your stand to allow motorists enough time to slow down. Signs detailing what you have for sale should be spaced 20-30 feet apart which will allow folks a chance to see everything you have to offer before they reach your stand.

And don't forget to advertise. If possible, advertise in your local newspaper and radio, particularly your first year. You can save on advertising by conducting gardening courses for people in the community, mentioning of course, your business as you teach. Also, to-the-point business cards can be printed up inexpensively. These can be distributed to potential customers in your locale.

Some county extension agencies print a directory of fresh produce stands and U-pick mom and pop businesses in their respective state. Be sure your business is included in this reference manual.

Finally, there's no better advertising than word of mouth. If you build a good business—offering fresh wholesome produce at reasonable prices—people **will** come.

REFERENCES

Sell what you sow; the Grower's Guide to Successful Produce Marketing by Eric Gipson, 1993.

The Maine Organic Farmer & Gardener July/August 1994, "Farmers Sell Marketing Ideas," by Paul Volckhausen. Comments at MOFGA'S 1993 FARMER TO FARMER CONFERENCE.

KIDS AND GARDENING

As I pulled into the driveway one warm afternoon in late August I observed—on the steps of my front porch—what looked like the aftermath of a tornado in a corn field. Sitting in the middle of this melee were my two daughters. I demanded to know what they were doing.

"We're "shicking" corn," they replied with a big grin.

This corn was special. Not only did they plant it in their own little garden, they were, er, shucking it so mommy could cook it for dinner.

Getting children involved in gardening can be fun and rewarding. It can also be a learning experience. It's a good way to teach children that corn, for example, doesn't "come from a can." It can also be a good way to get children to eat those "yucky" vegetables. When it comes time to harvest the garden they planted, hoed, watered and picked, they'll be anxious to try those yummy veggies.

Children learn to identify vegetables they grow themselves. Even a three year-old will quickly learn the names of several different vegetables. For the older child, labeling the rows will help her learn to recognize new words.

"Why do plants need water? Why are you putting that powder on them?" Be prepared to answer some questions from your children, which may require a little research on your part. This is a good time for a brief science lesson.

Getting Children Interested

To get your kids into the dirt (this really isn't hard!) pick a corner of the garden away from your more cherished and fragile plants. Acquire some tools for your children. However, don't waste your money on those plastic garden utensils found in the toy section of a department store. Kids will go after the soil with a

Allow children to use grown-up garden tools, not toy replicas.

vengeance, easily breaking these toy replicas. Some nurseries and hardware stores sell durable garden tools for children. Or take an old hoe and cut it down to size. The point is, be realistic. If you're going to let your children garden, let them do it for real, not pretend.

I also let them paint a sign to place in the middle of their garden patch. Children seem to have a need to know what belongs to them ("my toys, my bike"... you get the picture I'm sure). Besides, they'll be delighted seeing their names on a sign posted over their garden plot.

Children should help with seed selection. This way they feel more involved in the project. However, steer them towards larger seeds, such as, corn, beans and squash. Those tiny seeds, like carrot seed, may be too difficult for the budding green thumb to handle.

North Country Gardening
by Neil Moran

For that first garden experience, plant quick-germinating seeds: beans, radishes and peas. Immediate results will grab a child's attention much better than if she has to wait for weeks to see something come up.

With a little patience (for little gardeners) children can be taught to dig a furrow, properly space seeds and cover the seed up with the proper amount of soil. After the plants come up, show them how to cultivate and weed between rows and around hills they've planted. Also, let them pull weeds. This can be a little risky, of course, but it's the only way they'll learn how to distinguish between weeds and vegetable plants.

Expect mistakes, like the time my six-year old picked all of the green tomatoes. Boy, was she proud of her bounty! Despite the risks, however, it's important children be allowed to pick vegetables when they ripen; the only way they'll learn is by doing.

Gardening with children is fun. Besides swatting mosquitoes, it's a good pastime to keep you and the kids busy during the summer months.

And who knows, they may even start appreciating those "yucky" vegetables.

EXIBITING YOUR PRODUCE

There's no better reward for a season of hoeing and sowing than to see a blue ribbon dangling from your garden exhibit at a county fair. Entering garden exhibits at a county fair is a great way to share your garden successes with others and contribute to the many other interesting exhibits at the fair.

Over the years I've learned what the judges look for in a garden display. Although it probably varies with different judges, there are a few basics you must learn to achieve that blue ribbon quality.

Planning for a garden exhibit actually begins in the spring when you order your seeds. For individual exhibits, select your favorite easy-to-grow varieties. This will ensure you have ripe vegetables in time for the fair. Difficult-to-grow and unusual varieties are also good picks for a fair. For instance, you'll definitely impress the judges if you grow a 50 pound pumpkin in your northern garden!

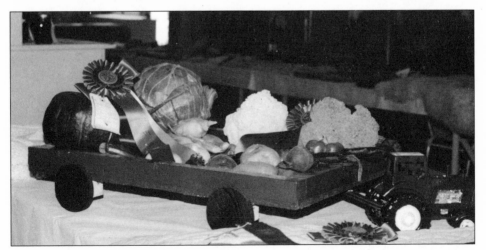

This garden display won the author a "Best of Show" at the Chippewa County Fair in Kinross, Michigan.

191

North Country Gardening

by Neil Moran

For a family garden display, the emphasis is on variety. You can enter all of the produce you normally plant in addition to some unusual or decorative vegetables, such as gourds or miniature pumpkins, which will add color and uniqueness to your display. Exhibit these on a miniature wheelbarrow or colored basket for an added touch.

Reserve your sunniest and most fertile spot in the garden for your potential garden exhibits. Plant early enough so your produce will be ready at fair time. I've had some difficulty, for instance, getting my squash and pumpkins ripe for our late August fair. I try to pamper my plants along by regular watering and fertilizing so they'll be ready when the time comes.

Like most aspects of gardening, a certain amount of time goes into selecting produce that has that blue ribbon quality. Here are a few surefire tips on selecting produce for display:

- Big is not always better. Select fruit that is attractive to the eye, has a nice shape and is ripe but not overly so.

- If exhibits call for more than one vegetable per display, such as a half dozen cukes, make sure the produce is uniform in size and shape.

- Produce must be clean. Scrub carrots and other root crops gently with a vegetable brush.

- Judges look for variety as well as quality in family garden exhibits. Throw in an herb or two such as dill or sage to increase the attractiveness of the display.

- How vegetables are displayed is as important as the quality of the fruit. Attractive baskets and plates will enhance the appearance of your exhibit and catch the judge's eye. Use your imagination.

If you've never entered vegetables in a county fair, you should consider doing so. Who knows, you may even win a ribbon. Of course, winning isn't everything. What you contribute to the fair will only add to the many interesting exhibits. And there's a sense of satisfaction seeing folks stopping to look at your prized vegetables.

SOURCES FOR SEEDS AND EQUIPMENT

The following companies either specialize in northern seeds and plants or offer hardy-for-the-north varieties.

VEGETABLES

Burpee
Attn: Order Department
300 Park Avenue
Warminster PA 18991-0001

Burrell's Better Seeds
P.O. Box 150
Rocky Ford CO 81067

Butterbrooke Farm
78 Barry Road
Oxford CT 06483
Send SASE

Ed Hume Seeds Inc.
P.O. Box 1450
Kent WA 98035
Catalog $1.00

Garden City Seeds
1324 Red Crow Rd.
Victor MT 49875-9713

Gleckler's Seedman
Metamora OH 43540
(largest collection of Native
 American squash)

Gurney's Seed & Nursery Co.
110 Capital Street
Yankton SD 57079

Harris Seeds
60 Saginaw Drive
P.O. Box 22960
Rochester NY 14692-2960

Henry Field's Seed & Nursery
Company
415 North Burnett
Shenandoah IA 51602

Johnny's Selected Seeds
Foss Hill Road
Albion ME O4910-9731

McFayden
Box 1800
Brando, MB
Canada R7a 6n4

Park Seed Co.
Cokesbury Rd.
Greenwood SC 29647

Pinetree Garden Seeds
P.O. Box 300
New Gloucester ME 04260

Ronniger's Seed Potatoes
Star Rt. 95
Moyie Springs ID 83845
(over 160 varieties)

Seeds Trust
High Altitude Gardens
P.O. Box 1048
Hailey ID 83333

Stokes Seeds Inc.
Box 548
Buffalo NY 14240

Vermont Bean Seed Co.
Garden Lane
Fair Haven VT 05743

Vesey Seeds, Ltd.
P.O. Box 9000
Calais ME 04619
(actually Canadian company)

Willhite Seed Co.
P.O. Box 23
Poolville TX 76487

North Country Gardening

by Neil Moran

HERBS & RARE SEEDS

Goodwin Creek Gardens
P.O. Box 83
Williams OR 97544

Nichols Garden Nursery
1190 North Pacific Highway
Albany OR

The Thyme Garden
20546-N Alsea Hwy.
Alsea OR 97324

Timmouth Channel Farm
Town Gwy 19, Box 428 B-NG
Timmouth VT 05773

FLOWERS

Breck's
U.S. Reservation Center
6523 North Galena Rd.
Peoria IL 61632

Cascade Daffodils
P.O. Box 10626
White Bear Lake MN 44110

Dutch Gardens
P.O. Box 200
Adelphia NJ 07710

Jackson and Perkins
1 Rose Lane Dept. 121
Medford OR 97501
(Source for quality roses known to do well in the North)

J.L. Hudson, Seedsman
PO Box 1058
Redwood City CA 94064
Catalog $1.00

Milaeger's Gardens

4838 Douglas Ave.
Racine WI 53402-2498
Catalog $1.00

The Roserie at Bayfields,
Box R(E), Waldoboro ME 04572
(Roses to zone 3)

WATER GARDENS

Northwest Landscape
Supply, Inc.
12500-132nd Ave. NE
Kirkland WA 98034

Paradise Water Gardens
114 May St.
Whitma, MA 02382
Catalog $3.00 (refundable)

Perry's Water Gardens
191 Leatherman Gap Rd.
Franklin NC 28734

Wildlife Nurseries, Inc.   Water
Gardening
P.O. Box 2724 NG
Oshkosh WI 54903
Catalog $3.00

William Tricker, Inc.
7125 Tanglewood Drive,
Dept. NG
Independence OH 44131
Catalog $2.00

FRUITS AND BERRIES
(may also sell vegetable seeds, flowers etc.)

Bear Creek Nursery
P.O. Box 411
Northport WA 99157

Farmer Seed and Nursery
818 Northwest 4th Street
Faribault MN 55021

Fedco Trees
Box 340
Palermo ME 04354

Johnson's Nursery
W180 N6275 Marcy Road
Menomonee Falls WI 53051

J.W. Jung Seed
335 South High Street
Randolph WI 43957

Keddy's Nursery
RR#1
Kentville, Nova Scotia
Canada B4N 3v7

Miller Nurseries
J.E. Miller Nurseries Inc.
5060 West Lake Road
Canandaigua NY 14424

Northwoods Nursery
28696 S. Cramer Rd.
Molalla OR 97038

SOURCE FOR WILD RICE

Manitok Wild Rice
c/o Dave Reinke
Box 97
Callaway MN 56521
1-800-726-1863

CKNOWLEDGEMENTS

- Betty Stover, a great friend of the family and former high school English teacher who proofread the section on flowers for me.

- Nancy and Ira McDonald, cottage gardeners in Grand Marais, Michigan, who spent a considerable amount of time with my wife and me in their gardens despite short notice. Nancy is Managing Editor of *"The American Cottage Gardener."* She offered advice for my section on flowers.

- Jerry and Janice Kessler, for their knowledge of greenhouses and starting plants from seeds. Janice has also given me a lot of encouragement along the way.

- Alan Alexander, from Erin, Ontario, for the excellent pictures and detailed explanation of his "glass cloche" method of gardening he brought over from England (I've also acquired a pen pal!).

- Ric and Shonna Vernagus, organic gardeners who not only shared their knowledge of plants and greenhouse gardening with me, but reminded me that you can garden without chemicals.

- Steve Fouch, Michigan State University Cooperative Extension Agent, for Chippewa and Emmet counties. Steve took time out of his busy schedule to fact check my section on trees and shrubs. His knowledge of northern cultivars and how to protect plants from our frigid winters was indispensable to this project.

- Steve Gregory, owner of Northscape Landscape Design in Sault Ste. Marie. He provided information on trees and shrubs. Steve's optimism and willingness to experiment with different cultivars in this region is contagious.

North Country Gardening

by Neil Moran

- Colleen Arbic, one of the first persons who encouraged me to write. This lady knows herbs and was willing to share her knowledge with me one winter day at "La Galerie," an antique and gift shop she owns in Sault Ste. Marie.

- Barbara Barker, owner of Willow Grove Farm in Brimley, Michigan. She was one of those people I stopped in on unannounced. However, she was more than willing to answer my questions on herb gardening.

- John Holm, nurseryman, plant breeder and horticulturist, in Alaska. You were too far away to talk with at any length; I'll have to come visit you some day.

- Grace and Roland Wurster, owners of Timbercrest Nursery in Marquette, Michigan. Thank you for your valuable assistance in different aspects of producing this book.

INDEX

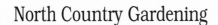

North Country Gardening

by Neil Moran

North Country Gardening

by Neil Moran

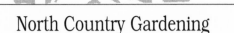

North Country Gardening

by Neil Moran